TAROT
For Christians
LESSONS FROM CHRIST'S FOOL

Archbishop Wynn Wagner

MYSTIC WAYS
BOOKS

Tarot for Christians: Lessons from Christ's Fool

ISBN 978-0-9855981-3-6

Mystic Ways Books
Dallas Texas 75219

www.HeckIfIKnow.com
www.WynnWagnerBooks.com
www.MysticWaysBooks.com

Bible quotations are taken from the King James edition (the translation that Jesus read).

Text quoted at length is in the public domain.

The sections called "A. E. Waite's Notes" are from *A Pictorial Key to the Tarot* by Arthur E. Waite (1911). It is the publication where Waite's ideas and Pamela Colman Smith's drawings first appeared together.

"We are fools for Christ's sake."
1 Corinthians 4:10

"The future isn't what it used to be."
Paul Valery (1871-1945)

"You can't connect the dots looking forward; you can only connect them looking backwards. So you have to trust that the dots will somehow connect in your future. You have to trust in something – your gut, destiny, life, karma, whatever. This approach has never let me down, and it has made all the difference in my life."
Steve Jobs (1955-2011)

Table of Contents

Introduction

"I WANT TO do a book about tarot," I told my agent.

Silence.

"Hello?" I said into the phone. "You still there?"

She hung up on me.

"You hung up on me," I said to her when I called back.

"No," she said. "I hung up on a crazy person who needs supervision."

"You don't want the book?"

"I don't know what to do with a book for Christians about tarot."

That's the reaction so many of us have. Tarot is a set of 78 pieces of rectangle cardstock and ink. You have 78 cartoon-like drawings, and we fear them like each one is done with some kind of material that is corrosive to the soul. If you're a proper Christian, you don't like the images or what they represent (regardless of what that might be).

The most popular deck in use today was drawn by a woman who specialized in illustrations for children's books. But we pack all kinds of overtones and innuendos and power and angst into these 78 sketches.

There was a time when I hated tarot. I was afraid of it because my family told me that hating the cards is what all good little Christians would do.

I was a good little Christian. Being a good boy is what made me want to live. It made me a solid member of the Christian community because I bound myself to the same rules and attitudes of everyone else.

When I questioned the order of things, my parents reminded me that I was just a kid. They said there were experts who denounced things like tarot. When I asked why, they told me it was obvious. They said that I was trying to "know better" than the really smart people who went to great schools and universities and had their names festooned with letters of honor: Reverend and Doctor and PhD and ThD and MA.

Nobody can know everything about everything. We had too many topics to master, and I should leave "fortune telling" alone because the experts said it was the devil's work. When I asked them were tarot was mentioned in the Bible, they got angry. They said I was inviting Satan into my soul.

They'd start quoting the Old Testament: "If a person turns to mediums and necromancers, whoring after them, I will set my face against that person and will cut him off from among his people." Leviticus is always the Go To Book for bigots and scalawags.

They warned me not to give tarot and astrology the time of day.

> *Now after Jesus was born in Bethlehem of Judea in the days of Herod the king, behold, wise men from the east came to Jerusalem, saying, "Where is he who has been born king of the Jews? For we saw his star when it rose and have come to worship him.*
>
> [Matthew 2:1-2]

Wait. What? The stars told the three wise men to come visit Jesus in the manger. They came to visit from the East. Holy men from the East. If I add up those numbers, carry the one, scrunch my eyes just so... the three wise men were actually astrologers, and they were coming from Persia (now Iran).

Mommy slapped me when I suggested that, of course. You can't "un-think" something like that. I knew the Magi were into astrology. Those sly Iranian geezers on camels were plotting the stars.

Mommy said it was better to accept their teaching on satanic things like tarot. They didn't want me to stir the pot.

"The best way to turn muddy water into clear water," she said, "is to leave it alone."

My ears always turn that kind of admonition into a dare.

Jesus founded two churches. Most people today know about the second one, but the original group is more fun.

Our Master hung out with all the wrong kinds of people during His earthly ministry.

He was a party guy. The first miracle passed down to us in the gospels was changing water into wine at a wedding celebration.

"Dude!" I imagine myself saying at that wedding party in Cana.[1]

Jesus hung with scoundrels and the sick and the scum of society. He cared about prisoners and kept crowds of bullies away from the disenfranchised.

Society hated them because they weren't up to society's standards. Followers of Jesus weren't proper people. They were riffraff, uneducated herds of ruffians. The hoi polloi.

I love rabble rousers. Jesus apparently fit in nicely. He was such an outsider that his own people had him murdered, killed by the upstanding citizens. They said he was such a criminal that he didn't deserve to live.

Constantine (272-337) started the second Christian church. He was the Roman emperor who first said Christianity was proper. He did it for political reasons more than anything.

Constantine told Roman society that it was okay to be a Christian. Citizens who wanted to suck up to the emperor left their non-Christian religions as fast as their brown-nosing chariots could race.

After politicians and middle-managers got their hands on the dogma, everything changed. The cross — Christianity's central symbol — went from a crude depiction of a dying man to a stylized figure in vestments and jewels.

I have lots of non-Christian friend. Many of them don't like "the church." It's like two camps, and they can't stand each other. What my non-Christian friends don't like is the second church of Constantine. I think lots of them would find our Master an absolute hoot. They'd like the liberal / pacifist / activist who partied with society's riffraff.

---

[1] Cana doesn't exist today. It was probably a village in what is Northern Israel.

My cousins fit into the second incarnation of the Christian church. I don't and never did.

I can see my cousins wince at the idea that their cousin would write a book suggesting that such a devil's tool as tarot could be useful, a set of meritorious flash cards with useful lessons to help us grow and flourish.

My cousins will be calling me a sorcerer over this book. If that's what they think, I will just turn the other cheek (or turn the other adverb, or whatever one turns in this situation). It isn't true. If I were a sorcerer, my cousins would be covered in warts by now. I won't correct them because I think it's cute. Also, it's a distinction that gives me the edge at family picnics and the invariable "discussions" at those outings.

Those of us who fit into the Master's original church group don't fit neatly into the second group.

"Don't talk to that heathen, Johnny," I can hear my cousins say. "He's evil."

The truth is far less dramatic. I use tarot as flash cards. They challenge my noggin without dragging words into the discussion. They are so jam-packed with imagery and symbols that there's an almost inexhaustible supply of novel facets that attack my preconceived assumptions about the spiritual world.

They're great, and they annoy my cousins, which makes them even more valuable.

Tarot speaks to the right side of my brain.

My left-brain gets assaulted with words and ideas from all kinds of places, but my artistic right-brain is ignored in my modern, internet-savvy daily life.

The left-brain is where engineers live. It's analytical and precise. It's so busy being accurate with the botany that it forgets to notice that a red rose is one of God's creations that deserves a standing ovation.

Tarot presents images — archetypes — to my right brain. It communicates with images instead of words. I see and recognize, without having to parse and translate.

The rose is just the rose.

The people who design tarot decks add titles at the bottom of each card: magician, devil, moon, and temperance. It sends those of us with left-brain afflictions into tailspins. Words on so many of the cards are just a ruse. We can get a hint about the meanings, but the minute we start taking those letters too seriously, the whole thing goes south.

I've more insights by staring at the images and letting my brain wander. When I see something that is in contradistinction to some expert's reality, the expert loses. Sorry, experts.

I've used tarot cards as flash cards since I was a little kid.

For years, I'd cut my tarot deck to select one card in the morning. It was my card of the day. I'd carry that card with me and stare at it when I had some downtime.

Some days I'd look at the card. Some days the card would look back at me. It was a dance.

When I'm writing one of my fictional novels, I get into a rut from time to time. My secret for writer's block: cut the tarot deck and select a card. It isn't that there is some kind of cosmic something-or-other going on. Maybe there is; maybe not. The point is that the image on the random card mounts an assault on my writer's block. The symbolism, the archetype, in the image shakes whatever was causing my mental constipation. It has worked over and over.

I did an actual tarot reading one time too. Once. It was sort of a reading. I laid out the cards and consulted a big book to see what each position was supposed to tell me. It was awful. I am the most inept prognosticator in the history of tarot. Every time I tried to take that reading seriously, I burst into laughter.

My guardian angel was laughing at me. Hosts of cherubim and seraphim were laughing so hard that they started passing gas, and that isn't a pretty thing to happen.

As a result of that reading, I swore off the practice.

If you want to learn how to "read" the cards and tell the future, I'm not the one to come to. I haven't any advice.

What's more, I don't think the future is any of my business.

The past is the past. It doesn't even exist. The only way we can interact with the past is to think about it, and that thinking is happening NOW. Bad thoughts about the past include shame and regret. Those are just thoughts, and they can ruin the present.

Same thing for the future. It doesn't exist. We can only think about it, and our thinking happens NOW. Bad thoughts of the future can be dread and fear, but they're just thought patters. The future doesn't exist, and our bad thought only muck up the present.

If you want to get your head off into the future, that's all up to you. I have enough trouble with NOW. Adding time-shifts to my NOW complicates things beyond pleasure.

So Many Decks

TAROT DECKS TODAY range from angel cards and wildwood cards to Osho Zen and Rider-Waite. The most popular is Rider-Waite, and even that has a boatload of spinoffs: Albano-Waite, Morgan Greer, and Universal Tarot are just a few. The derivative decks show that (a) there's money to be made, and (b) designers think they can improve on the original Rider-Waite images.

In addition to the mass-market decks, artists produce one-of-a-kind decks. Some of these can cost hundreds or thousands of dollars.

A deck doesn't have to be strange or expensive. It doesn't have to be in some kind of niche to be useful. We are going to explore one of the garden-variety decks.

Arthur Waite and Pamela Smith sold rights to their tarot deck to the Rider Company. Today Rider is a subsidiary or imprint of Random House, but back then it was a fledgling printer of occult books in Britain.

We had two distinctions in 1909: the Wait-Smith tarot deck, and plastic.

Pamela Smith did all the artwork for the cards. They were based on some notes from Arthur Waite. Somehow when they started handing out credit for the cards, the boys somehow forgot to include Miss Smith when they were peeing on their tarot fire hydrants.

In 1971, U.S. Games published a version of Rider's tarot cards. When you see a deck for sale today, it is probably from U.S. Games. If it has cards that look like the ones drawn by Pamela Smith, it's probably called Rider-Waite.

We are going to call this deck, the Waite-Smith deck because the only real contribution to the project on the part of Rider was a few of pails of ink and some card stock.

Pamela ("Pixie") Colman Smith

She was Pixie to her friends, but she was born Corinne Pamela Colman Smith near London in 1878. Her dad was a lawyer from Brooklyn, New York. Some say that Pixie's mother came from Jamaica, but there's little actual evidence of that.

Her parents called her Pam when she was a kid and Miss Smith after she grew up. In addition to London, young Pam/Pixie/Pamela/Miss Smith also spent time in Manchester in northern England.

Figure 1: Pixie Smith

They eventually moved to Jamaica, and young Pixie soaked up so much of the local lore that she was able to write and illustrate books about Jamaica folklore.

Her mother's family was all about children's books. Her grandmother and a couple of aunts wrote them, so nobody was surprised when young Pamela showed an early talent with children's books. She has several to her name, including the *Annancy Stories*, which combines her love of Jamaican folklore with children's stories.

She met and became friends with Bram Stoker and William Butler Yeats, and she was the illustrator for some of their works. [e.g., Stoker's Sir Henry Irving and several magazine articles from Yeats].

Pixie Smith met Arthur Edward Waite at a bookstore in London. She was there to promote one of her books, and Watkin's Books was a gathering place for those interested in "alternative" spirituality. At the store, she met Bram Stoker (1847-1912), William Wynn Westcott (1848-1925), MacGregor Mathers (1854-1918), Arthur Edward Waite (1857-1942), and Aleister Crowley (1875-1947).

She was an active adherent of the Roman Catholic Church.

ARTHUR EDWARD WAITE

Arthur Edward Waite wanted to write poetry, which is like saying you want to starve to death. Thanks to an education in a private school near London, he was able to support himself as a clerk while trying to write the poem that would make him rich and famous. We don't really remember him for his verse, so that aspect didn't work out like he had hoped.

Figure 2: A. E. Waite in 1921

A. E. Waite was born in 1857 in England. His mother raised her kids as Roman Catholics, which wasn't the most common option in Anglican England.

Waite's sister died when he was only a teenager. He was devastated.

The death made him start exploring things outside the mainstream. Society didn't give him the answers he sought, so he started on a quest to see the unseen. He was a Freemason and a member of the Golden Dawn.

He took a scholarly approach to mysticism and the occult.

THE WAITE-SMITH DECK

In 1907, the Sola Busca family of Italy that owned the only complete (78-card) tarot deck from the 15th century, commissioned some black-and-white photos of their prized heirloom. One set of prints was presented to the British Museum. The photographs were put on display, to the delight of all the Brits who were interested in the occult. That included Pamela Colman Smith and Arthur Edward Waite.

If there's any specific proof that Miss Smith took her sketchbook to the exhibit, I haven't seen it. That said, a side-by-side comparison of the cards reveals that the Sola Busca deck from 1491 was the major influence on the Waite-Smith deck of the 20th century.

When Arthur Waite and Pamela Smith talked about the Sola Busca deck, they knew they could modernize the images. Waite was a walking encyclopedia of myth and symbolism, and so he outlined the main points of the major arcana[2] (the 22 named cards, not the 56 pip or suit cards). Waite's notes were all Miss Smith needed to get started.

Within a few months, the pair had a complete set of drawings for the entire deck. Each card was true to the symbolism generally accepted by Golden Dawn members of the time.

Miss Smith based her major arcana on the notes from A. E. Waite. She did the minor arcana on her own.

The occultist, Aleister Crowley, hated the Waite-Smith deck, by the way. He didn't like Waite or his tarot and wrote about both several times. Crowley eventually produced his own tarot, called the Thoth Tarot. If Thoth speaks to you, God bless you for it. It's just me, but I find Crowley's tarot deck to be about as useful as an ashtray on a motorcycle.

There is another deck of note: Le Tarot de Marseille. It probably dates to the 1400s, like the Sola Busca deck. Marseille has plenty of fans. I like the deck, too, but my choice for this book is the one drawn in the 20th century by Pixie Smith. In a way, the drawings in Marseille are more organic and subtle. Smith was an illustrator, mainly of children's books. I think Marseille offers great mental images, but I like the simplicity and clarity in Smith's drawings. (Your mileage may vary.)

---

[2] ar·ca·num [ahr-key-nuhm] noun, (plural ar·ca·na [-nuh]) a secret or mystery. ORIGIN mid 16th century: from Latin, neuter plural of *arcanus*.

Card O. The Fool

> *For the message of the cross is foolishness to those who are perishing, but to us who are being saved it is the power of God.*
>
> [1 Corinthians 1:18]

When God asks you to walk off a metaphorical cliff, you can assume one of two things will happen. Either there is an unseen ledge just below the scary edge, or you will be given the ability to fly.

Alcoholics Anonymous and other 12-Step programs say we have to "hit bottom" before there can be any kind of "recovery." Whether we suffer from addiction or just the pains of life itself, we have to continue trying things our way until the universe convinces us that it's bigger than we are. We have to let go of things. Absolutely let go of everything.

Recovery is an extreme process. Unless you really get to the point where you know you can't drink and know you can't stop, you haven't visited that strange untenable place where there's no solution.

A friend of mine who was trying to get sober wanted to get it done right, so he made a list of things he would be turning over to God. His hand gave out, so he just listed the things he was supposed to keep. It was a short list. In fact, the only thing my friend was convinced would have to be on his Keep List: willingness. He couldn't even turn over the act of turning things over.

People who haven't found their personal bottom rarely understand. They say you can't let go absolutely. They say that you have to control things. You have to pay your taxes and make a living, and that means we need to be in charge of our own destiny.

Those who have lived through a personal holocaust will tell you otherwise.

> *And why are you worried about clothing? Observe how the lilies of the field grow; they do not toil nor do they spin, yet I say to you that not even Solomon in all his glory clothed himself like one of these. But if God so clothes the grass of the field, which is alive today and tomorrow is thrown into the furnace, will He not much more clothe you? You of little faith!* [Matthew 6:28-30]

Siddhartha Gautama (c486 BCE - c483 BCE) wanted enlightenment. The Indian prince wanted to understand. He needed to understand. He decided to sit under a tree until he was enlightened. He sat and sat. After a month and a half, he did the one thing that we all have to do. Gautama gave up, and in that split second his enlightenment appeared. He became the Buddha when he gave up.

Thomas Merton (1915-1968) says that his silent contemplation as a monk was anything but tranquil. It made him empty himself of everything — good and bad — to let him present his empty soul to God.

> *The worst of it is that even apparently holy conceptions are consumed along with all the rest. it is a terrible breaking and burning of idols, a purification of the sanctuary, so that no graven thing may occupy the place that God has commanded to be left empty.*
> [New Seeds of Contemplation, Thomas Merton]

But we don't see it. Think of a glass — crystal or paper or styrofoam. It's probably round, and it may be colored. That isn't the working part of the glass. The part of a glass we really use is the big hole of air. If somebody offers you wine, you don't present a glass full of water (not even if it is expensive designer water). You hold up an empty glass.

THE FOOL card is number zero.

Zero is a bona fide digit. It isn't the absence of number'ness. In fact, when computers count things, the first instance is number zero. The first slot in an array of widgets is slot zero. If you haven't counted your widgets (you poor widget'less urchin), a computer would reckon that as "quantity = nil". The absence of the number zero is different from zero itself. So in computers, a zero is —

1. the first instance in an array (slot zero)
2. zero (quantity)

3. the absence of a number (we haven't counted the widgets, and that's different from not having any)

Not-zero is NAN ("not a number") to computers, and that's usually stored as an impossibly weird negative number with a gazillion digits after a fictitious decimal place. Computers don't really have the concept of "not-zero" so engineers had to invent a spectacularly arcane way of storing such a concept. To the computer, NAN is just a number. Something between the computer chips and the human eyeball is something that recognizes this special "number" and replaces it with NAN. And if the computer runs across this strange representation outside of its meaning as NAN, we are in serious trouble. We have NAN and a number all in one. It may rip holes in the universe.

Forget the computer for a second. It doesn't know about NANs, not natively.

When you see "0" on the Fool's card, it is the first card of the deck. It isn't the number zero! This "0" is really a NAN. It is Merton's empty soul. It is the Buddha giving up. It is the alcoholic giving up. It is the empty wine glass.

Think of your favorite food. It is a wonderful treat, this whatever-it-is.

Mine is a medium rare ribeye steak with a little crustiness on the outside, charred by the heat of a grill of mesquite or pecan wood. I am drooling on my keyboard right now.

That isn't NAN! Even though my favorite food is complete awesomeness, it is just the opposite of what The Fool card represents. In this exercise, we are going for emptiness. We are presenting God an empty glass. Not even the best liquid can be in the goblet. It has to be empty.

Now I think of that ribeye steak in the fraction of a second before my mind kicks in. It is the steak before I recognize the flavor and aroma and appearance. It just is. It is the steak without modifier or prejudice.

Your favorite food just is. Before you recognize it, the food merely exists. It is what philosophers call "undifferentiated." The food is simply itself. It isn't nourishment or non-nourishment. It isn't good or awesome or hideous. Your highly developed brain hasn't put it into any of its zillion cubby holes. It is what it is.

Some (but not all) Kabalists say that The Fool is associated with malkuth, which is the lowest circle or ball on the Kabalistic Tree of Life. It is the root of Kabala, but it isn't spiritual or non-spiritual. It isn't God or not-God. It isn't ribeye or not-ribeye (although I can't understand why anybody would be so extreme as to embrace not-ribeye). It just is, without decoration or adjectives.

The Fool isn't foolish. It is emptiness.

In the card, our hero is marching headlong off a cliff while his dog screams out warnings.

"Ruff, ruff," says the dog. "Fool overboard! Ruff, ruff."

The Fool just walks.

Saint Symeon Salus (a.k.a. Simeon, a.k.a. Weird Holy Dude)

The Fool is like Saint Symeon Salus (? – 570 AD) of the Roman Church. He lived in a cave for thirty years, subsisting on lentils and water.[3] When he left the cave, he walked to Emesa in Syria. Symeon could be found dragging dead animals around or throwing nuts at the clergy and blowing out the altar candles. On some days when adherents were to fast, Symeon would eat huge quantities of beans. (Oh, yes he did) The town's fuddy duddies wanted to run out of town because of all the farts. After he died, the townspeople reflected on his antics. He really was saintly, chopping the pompous down to size. That time he broke a young man's jaw had kept the man from starting an adulterous relationship.

Saint Symeon played the fool and was bullied for it. On his deathbed, Symeon gave his life-long friend John some sage[4] advice that is one of the most important saint-quotes I've ever seen. He said,

---

[3] Can you even imagine? If he wasn't The Fool before this regimen... this is your brain... this is your brain on lentils....

[4] I can just hear Symeon with a retort that it is parsley advice, not sage.

> *I beg you, never disregard a single soul, especially when it happens to be a monk or a beggar. For your charity knows that His place is among the beggars, especially among the blind, people made as pure as the sun through their patience and distress.... Show love of your neighbor through almsgiving. For this virtue, above all, will help us on (the Day of Judgment).*[5]   [Saint Symeon]

> *The foolish things of the world to shame the wise; the weak things of the world to shame the strong.*   [1 Corinthians 1:27]

BEGGAR

Older decks show The Fool as a beggar, like the Buddhist monk who carries a begging bowl for daily nourishment.

In the Smith-Waite deck, the fool is carrying a white rose, a sign of purity. Roses can smell nice (good) but grabbing them willy-nilly gets you an introduction to their prickers (bad). We haven't seen the last of the rose symbolism in the tarot deck. They also festoon The Magician, Strength, and Death.

WHITE ROSE

The Fool has the rose in his left hand, and that's a traditional symbol for receptive energies.

Most people are right-handed, and artists who use symbolism use that fact. When they draw a right hand pointing, it's to punch some emotion or attitude coming out of the person. The left hand is just the opposite. Symbolic artists use the left hand to tell us that the person is receiving something. In this case, it's the purity of a white rose.

The fool isn't foolish here because he's holding it delicately between his thumb and first finger to avoid the thorns. He is holding the good and the bad lightly, "wearing" the rose like a loose-fitting garment.

---

[5] Krueger, Derek. *Symeon the Holy Fool*. U.C. Berkeley, 1996. §7.

א

The Fool is often linked to the Hebrew letter Aleph (א). If any-thing, Arthur Waite was an organized mystic. He charted everything. He liked everything in its proper place. Showing that the Fool has an affinity to a particular letter in a foreign alphabet is something he loved to do. In this case, the alphabet is Hebrew, and people interest-ed in esoteric philosophy have been assigning meanings and associa-tions to Hebrew letters for thousands of years.

Aleph is the first letter of the Hebrew alphabet. The letter also appears in Arabic, Syriac, and even ancient Phoenician alphabets. It is one of the few written vowels in those languages, and that's a hard-ship on readers. Arabic, for example, can have the same letters to mean peace (silm) and ladder (sullam). Sometimes the reader has to backtrack, especially after realizing that an anti-war protester proba-bly wouldn't be giving a speech on ladders.

Modern writing in Arabic and Hebrew adds dots, strategically placed to tell the reader about the vowels.

In ancient Egypt, their phonetic glyphs had no vowels whatsoev-er. Not even Aleph. It's why we only have some educated guesses on what the ancient words sounded like.

Here's history's nasty little secret about alphabets: all those an-cient people were good-for-nothings too lazy to write out the full word. (just kidding)

The truth is that the... I mean... okay, nobody knows. Experts from fancy schools with pedigrees sit around arguing with each other about this. People who study ancient languages can't agree on a rea-son for those languages banishing vowels.

- Some say it's wrapped up in the ancient notion that if you know someone's name, you can be a mystical bully over that person.
- Others say they didn't need vowels because "everybody knew" what the words sounded like. Writing was to dis-

tinguish a scorpion from a rock in a story, not to document the spoken language.

The Fool card is Aleph, and that means card Zero is the first breath of tarot.

Breath is the thing that connects every living creature on earth. We all breathe, whether it is air through lungs or water through gills. It is our way of sharing our surroundings in a very fundamental way.

Aleph is the breath that starts Semitic alphabets. It is life itself, completely shared but neither good nor bad.

> *The disciples came and said to Him, "Why do you speak to them in parables?"*
>
> *He answered and said to them, "Because it has been given to you to know the mysteries of the kingdom of heaven, but to them it has not been given. For whoever has, to him more will be given, and he will have abundance; but whoever does not have, even what he has will be taken away from him. Therefore I speak to them in parables, because seeing they do not see, and hearing they do not hear, nor do they understand. And in them the prophecy of Isaiah is fulfilled, which says:*
>
> *'Hearing you will hear and shall not understand, And seeing you will see and not perceive; For the hearts of this people have grown dull. Their ears are hard of hearing, And their eyes they have closed, Lest they should see with their eyes and hear with their ears, Lest they should understand with their hearts and turn, So that I should heal them.'*
>
> *"But blessed are your eyes for they see, and your ears for they hear; for assuredly, I say to you that many prophets and righteous men desired to see what you see, and did not see it, and to hear what you hear, and did not hear it.*   [Matthew 13:10-17]

Pray for us, Saint Symeon Salus, that we may be *serious without being solemn*... that we may plunge ahead, damn the torpedoes... four bells, captain. Wait... torpedoes? Holy moly. Abandon ship. Authors first.

A. E. WAITE'S NOTES ON THE FOOL

With light step, as if earth and its trammels had little power to restrain him, a young man in gorgeous vestments pauses at the brink of a precipice among the great heights of the world; he surveys the blue distance before him-its expanse of sky rather than the prospect below. His act of eager walking is still indicated, though he is stationary at the given moment; his dog is still bounding. The edge, which opens on the depth, has no terror; it is as if angels were waiting to uphold him, if it came about that he leaped from the height. His countenance is full of intelligence and expectant dream. He has a rose in one hand and in the other a costly wand, from which depends over his right shoulder a wallet curiously embroidered. He is a prince of the other world on his travels through this one-all amidst the morning glory, in the keen air. The sun, which shines behind him, knows whence he came, whither he is going, and how he will return by another path after many days. He is the spirit in search of experience. Many symbols of the Instituted Mysteries are summarized in this card, which reverses, under high warrants, all the confusions that have preceded it.

In his Manual of Cartomancy,[6] Grand Orient[7] has a curious suggestion of the office of Mystic Fool, as apart of his process in higher divination; but it might call for more than ordinary gifts to put it into operation. We shall see how the card fares according to the common arts of fortune-telling, and it will be an example, to those who can discern, of the fact, otherwise so evident, that the Trumps Major had no place originally in the arts of psychic gambling, when cards are used as the counters and pretexts. Of the circumstances under which this art arose we know, however, very little. The conventional explanations say that the Fool signifies the flesh, the sensitive life, and by a peculiar satire its subsidiary name was at one time the alchemist, as depicting folly at the most insensate stage.

---

[6] Fortune telling using randomly selected playing cards.

[7] A jurisdiction or authority in Freemasonry.

Card 1. The Magician

> *Do not love the world or the things in the world. If anyone loves the world, the love of the Father is not in him. For all that is in the world — the desires of the flesh and the desires of the eyes and pride in possessions — is not from the Father but is from the world. And the world is passing away along with its desires, but whoever does the will of God abides forever.* [1 John 2:15-17]

The journey of our fool begins in the last place you might expect. We have an innocent vagabond, ignoring the panicked barks of his dog, prancing right off a cliff. The first stop of the fool's journey is in a place where he has absolutely everything.

The Magician holds a wand (fire) in front of a table with a coin (earth), sword (air), and chalice (water). Those are the four basic elements of the ancients. They didn't need the granularity they teach our kids today. They were okay not being up-to-speed on the differences between berkelium and arsenic. They didn't know about neon, which explains why they didn't have blinking lights advertising the sphinx.

The "one" card is actually the second card in the deck, and it's big claim to fame is how it presents the four elements. You can drown in all the digits here.

Four elements. Christians have four official gospels. The person who fought hardest for Matthew, Mark, Luke, and John was a cleric named Irenaeus (130-202):

> *The Gospels could not possibly be either more or less in number than they are. Since there are four zones of the world in which we live, and four principal winds, while the Church is spread over all the earth, and the pillar and foundation of the Church is the gospel, and the Spirit of life, it fittingly has four pillars, everywhere breathing out incorruption and revivifying men.*
> [Irenaeus, *Adversus Haereses*, 3.3.3]

Of course there are four gospels because there are four directions and four winds.

Water has a solid direction: down. If you try to get it to stand upright, it will ignore you. It will completely cover the lowest point it can get to. At room temperature, water feels soft. Tell that to somebody caught in a great wave. Try to tell that to the rocks of a canyon that have been worn away by the impact of this "soft" alchemical element. When liquid behaves badly, we sometimes call it phlegm. Water is sometimes represented by a chalice. When an angel appears with water, it's often Gabriel.

 Earth is one of the four classic elements. Our over-expanded minds know that earth is a complex system of iron and uranium and horseradish. When it is soil or dust, earth will form to its container but not so reliably as water. The direction for earth is down, but it just sits around. Water forcibly goes down, like Niagara or Victoria Falls. Coins (pentagram) represent the element of earth in mystical drawings. If you spot an archangel loitering around earth, it's probably Uriel. Earth seems solid. It isn't, but it feels strong. There's a lot of it. We grow food in, and we walk all over it. Earth takes it all in stride.

 Air is just up there. We don't usually feel it moving itself to be on top of earth, but that's where to find it. "Direction" isn't severe like down is associated with water. A Greek philosopher in the 5th century BCE taught that air is somehow linked to intelligence. That means, we've been yapping about "air heads" for 2,500 years! Air surrounds us, but even the ancient philosophers knew it wasn't to be found between the stars and planets. Aristotle (384-322 BCE) used the term aether for the goo that held the planets together, and it had nothing to do with air. If there's an archangel in a mystic drawing of air, it's most likely Raphael. Air keeps us alive, and the breath of life is what connects us with other people (and dogs and butterflies). It also hoists the aroma of a ribeye steak. Mmmm.

Fire has an absolute direction: up. You can put your hand to each side of a lit candle. It's warm, but it isn't necessarily uncomfortable. If you put your palm the same distance from the flame but above it, you'll be screaming like a stuck pig in no time. The alchemical symbol for fire is the upward pointing triangle to show that fire wants to go straight up. Air can make a flame flicker, but the flame really wants to go straight up. Fire destroys and transforms. It changes water to steam. It changes rough metal into hardened steel. The archangel of fire is Michael, heaven's "fiery" hell raiser.

Our vagabond from Card Zero is a player, the central actor in his personal narrative. He's on an adventure. He's also an adept player of dungeons and dragons, which may be why he is starting with an exploration of the four basic weapons of the game. He has air and fire, water and earth. They are the building blocks of life, and The Fool has them all in equal measure.

Some people approach The Magician card like he represents control and power. Heavens, no! He represents balance.

Back in college, I took a course in photojournalism. We had cameras and actual film. Film! That same year, I took computer programming, and lab time consisted of me putting holes in punch cards. In other words, this was a very long time ago.

The photography teacher talked us through all the equipment on the first day of class. At our second meeting, we did absolutely everything. We loaded film into our cameras in total darkness; we exposed an entire roll of black-and-white film in snapshots of whatever was handy; we developed the film in the darkroom; we picked our favorite picture and made a 5-inch by 7-inch enlargement. Everything.

The teacher shocked us all at the start of the third class period.

"We aren't going to learn anything new from what you did last week," she said. "You did everything. What we're going to be doing for the rest of the semester is get good at what you already know how to do."

And that's exactly what we did. We built on the techniques and tools from that early class session. We polished what we had already learned.

Our Fool's adventure starts with The Magician. It includes all four of the elements recognized in the ancient world. He already has all the tools he will need as an alchemist. Four elements in equal measure.

I know what you're thinking: "How can I be part of an adventure that ignores Manganese, Iridium, and Barium?"

I say that sodium and uranium can kill you, dude. Just be happy we are summarizing the elements.

The sword on The Magician card isn't the main element. There aren't any main elements. The chalice is as important as the coin.

Look at Pixie Smith's magician, and you trip over the symbolism.

There's an infinity symbol (lemniscate) over his head and his belt is a serpent eating its own tail (uroboros). What I take from the double-whammy of infinity is that life goes on but doesn't always change.

Figure 3: lemniscate

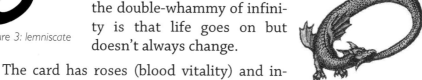

The card has roses (blood vitality) and introduces white lilies (purity).

Figure 4: uroboros

There are two other aspects that you only get by staring at this card for several years.

ONE

First, the magician isn't powerful. He's an engineer or a technician. The magician moves the elements around when requested to do so. He doesn't own the sword or the element of air it represents.

When he takes a long weekend, the magician stores his tools in a chest because he knows they're just tools. They aren't life itself. If the king and queen don't need energies moved around, most magicians wouldn't move the energies.

Our magician is young and cute. If he's supposed to come across as arcane and secretive and scary, I don't see it. This guy is somebody I might like to date, not run from.

Two

The second less-than-obvious aspect of The Magician card centers on his right hand.

At I used to think that the magician was receiving heaven's energies and transmitting them down to us on earth. In fact, he's doing just the opposite.

To any artist who knows about archetypes and symbolism, the right hand is the emitter. We saw this in The Fool holding a rose by the left hand.

Left hands always absorb, and right hands transmit.

When I saw this, it was like the sly magician turned upside-down and backwards. His absorbing hand points to earth. His right hand is emitting energies to heaven, and the wand in his right hand strengthens that idea. Wands are used symbolically be sorcerers to concentrate an energy flow. Instead of a cloud of intent, the sorcerer would be using a kind of metaphysical laser.

I started wondering what the magician might be sending out through his hand and wand, and I came up with a blank. I didn't give up on thinking that through. It really is a blank. The magician doesn't make up new elements. He just does what he's asked to do.

The magician picks up energies from one place and moves them somewhere else. He doesn't comment or modify those energies because that's not what a technician does. He doesn't try to make the energies prettier or more useful. The computer programmer doesn't change the fundamental hardware underlying the craft of programming. Software can't make your computer's case blue. No program makes your keyboard taste like chocolate or lingonberries. The programmer casts a spell over a collection of electrons. The programmer sends lasers of current, electrons flying in close formation to one another.

And what are the programmer's electrons doing? It's a blank. It doesn't matter to the programmer.

If you have a bucket of numbers and want them all lined up and multiplied and shifted and collated, you need to get yourself a computer programmer. Are the numbers better after the programmer finishes? No. Does the programmer change "3" into "4"? No, the programmer can combine "3" and "1" to come up with a four but no programmer can change the fundamental number itself.

ENGINEERING THE SOUL

The Fool's adventure makes its first stop in the class of that photography instructor. We get a full load of implements in the first card. We don't need to pickup anything more for our journey.

And if we're smart, we'll keep the attitude of the computer programmer. The magician moves things and collates things, but that doesn't make him powerful. It makes him crafty.

RULES OF THUMB FOR TOOLS

A razor blade may be the sharpest cutting device in your home, but it isn't going to work if you need to chop down a tree. The right tool works better.

You may have an awesome hammer in your tools, and it may be the heaviest hammer you could afford. That hammer is not going to let you nail a 6-inch nail into a piece of oak in one stroke. Persistence with the correct tool is the only thing that works.

If you're building a table to hold a fish tank, your most important tool is the level. If the aquarium stand isn't level, the tank isn't going to hold the right amount of water. You may have an artistic idea about what will look best, but accuracy is sometimes more important than creativity.

A. E. WAITE'S NOTES ON THE MAGICIAN

A youthful figure in the robe of a magician, having the countenance of divine Apollo, with smile of confidence and shining eyes. Above his head is the mysterious sign of the Holy Spirit, the sign of life, like an endless cord, forming the figure 8 in a horizontal position. About his waist is a serpent-cincture, the serpent appearing to devour its own tail. This is familiar to most as a conventional symbol of eternity, but here it indicates more especially the eternity of attainment in the spirit. In the Magician's right hand is a wand raised towards heaven, while the left hand is pointing to the earth. This dual sign is known in very high grades of the Instituted Mysteries; it shews the descent of grace, virtue and light, drawn from things above and derived to things below. The suggestion throughout is therefore the possession and communication of the Powers and Gifts of the Spirit. On the table in front of the Magician are the symbols of the four Tarot suits, signifying the elements of natural life, which lie like counters before the adept, and he adapts them as he wills.

Beneath are roses and lilies, the flos campi[8] and lilium convallium,[9] changed into garden flowers, to shew the culture of aspiration. This card signifies the divine motive in man, reflecting God, the will in the liberation of its union with that which is above. It is also the unity of individual being on all planes, and in a very high sense it is thought, in the fixation thereof.

With further reference to what I have called the sign of life and its connection with the number 8, it may be remembered that Christian Gnosticism speaks of rebirth in Christ as a change "unto the Ogdoad."

The mystic number is termed Jerusalem above, the Land flowing with Milk and Honey, the Holy Spirit and the Land of the Lord. According to Martinism,[10] 8 is the number of Christ.

---

[8] Flower of the field

[9] Lily of the valley

[10] A group of esoteric Christians that seek to find illumination for mankind, reintegrating all people back into the Eternal One.

Card 2. The Priestess

She sits erect with a crescent moon at her feet. She is framed by two stone columns called Boaz and Jachin, just like columns from the first temple in Jerusalem. The columns were on the front porch of Solomon's temple.

> *And concerning the pillars, the height of one pillar was eighteen cubits; and a fillet of twelve cubits did compass it; and the thickness thereof was four fingers: it was hollow. And a chapiter of brass was upon it; and the height of one chapiter was five cubits, with network and pomegranates upon the chapiters round about, all of brass. The second pillar also and the pomegranates were like unto these.*
> [Jeremiah 52:21-22]

A chapiter is a capital, the topmost part of a column. Our tarot chapiters are some kind of lotus motif with tasteful art deco decoration. The pomegranates seemed to have been banished to a veil strung between the columns.

The columns make several appearances in Saint Peter's Basilica in the Vatican. The pope's columns twist upwards in a kind of corkscrew, a style known as Solomonic columns.

So you get a couple of columns at Jerusalem's first temple. They appear again in Rome (although the popes didn't understand the symbolism of limiting the count to two columns). Pixie Smith used them again in her Priestess card.

You get a good design, and it's copied over and over.

Boaz was a military guy. Very Old Testament. Very Spanish Inquisition. Boaz represents blood and strength. Some say naming one of the columns Boaz was actually a shout-out to King David, the king who was so blood-thirsty that God wouldn't let him build the first temple [1 Chronicles 22:8]. David's son, Solomon, built the temple. God didn't reject David: He merely made it so we don't remember The Warrior's Temple. David could do lots of things besides building the temple.

The temple was a bloody place even without having David as the builder. Tons of animals lost their lives in sacrifices over the years.

David's son was the builder of the first temple, and that's commemorated in the column called Jachin. It is the column of the establisher, the builder. The word goes a little further than just involving Solomon. We get the establishment part from "chin." The other part — "Ja" — is a shortened form of one of Hebrew's names of God, Yahweh. So Jachin really is there to remind us that Yahweh is the establisher.

If you look closely between the veil and the columns, you can pot a sliver of something in the distance. It's probably an ocean. If she really annoyed The Magician, it could possibly be a big tsunami coming to rip down the pretty veil.

> And beneath upon the hem of [the robe] *thou shalt make pomegranates of blue, and of purple, and of scarlet, round about the hem thereof; and bells of gold between them round about.*
> [Exodus 28:33]

God is handing out instructions on the attire for Aaron, so he can be a priest. If God wants you accessorized a certain way, don't ask questions. Right?

In this case, pomegranates are used to show how fertile the Promised Land is. There are other stories that say a pomegranate was the evil fruit that got Adam and Eve in hot water with the landlord.

Lush growth in fertile soil are the meaning I take away from The Priestess card. Solomon describes his bride's "temples are like a piece of a pomegranate within thy locks." [Song of Solomon 4:3]

The bride's temples are hidden, secured by locks.

On our tarot card, the pomegranate (temples, fertile) are on a veil (locks, hidden, inner secrets) that is stretched between Boaz (blood-force) and Jachin (establishment of Yahweh). There are palm branches on the veil too.

And the veil is hiding mental insights that can be a day on the ocean's beach or the destruction of a tidal wave.

On her head, she has a hat that reminds us of moon phases: waxing, full, and waning. The moon is all here, but she isn't telling us the whole story.

In the priestess's lap is a scroll with writing that says it is the Torah, a holy book of Judaism. The scroll is partially hidden. A Jewish priestess with ties to Solomon's temple? I think not.

She is rigid, and her skin modestly hidden. He robe covers everything except her face and one hand. A cape seems to constrain the priestess's arms.

She's a little rigid to my eyes. The poor woman is sitting so erect that I think somebody seems to have put Velcro or duct tape to keep her motionless against the chair. It isn't like she's relaxing in front of a television or reposting photos on Facebook.

Is she being proper, or has somebody got her in bondage?

The contrast is so sharp between the woman's posture and her flowing robe. It's blue and poofy. It almost looks like her gown changes into a waterfall as you look towards the bottom of the card.

That's exactly what Mr. Waite and Miss Smith want you to see. This is the first appearance of moving water that will pop up time and again in other cards.

The flowing water even trickles over the crescent moon.

Water is fundamental to myths and religions. The original goo of the universe is described as the primordial waters. One fundamental theme with the ancient Egyptians was the waters of the Nile, which flooded and fertilized their fields.

Water fills its container perfectly. If you put it into a round glass, you have round water. No conversion is required to get it to fit in a square bucket. It is soft to the touch when it's a room temperature, but flowing water can cut through rocks better than almost anything else.

We are going to see water over and over in the subsequent cards.

There's an old method of creating "moon water." You take a bowl of water outside during a full moon. With an eyedropper you pull water out of the part of the bowl where you see the moon's reflection.

Its affinity is to the feminine aspect of God. It is God as Mother, nurturing and loving. Some even put a silver coin in the bowl to heighten the reflection.

That's the operative word, by the way: reflection. Water reflects light. The moon reflects light. Moon water comes from the reflection of a reflection, and I don't know how you get deeper into philosophy than that.

Our adventurer — nobody's fool, really — takes the same initial steps so many of us do. We read and study. We reflect the ideas of others. The priestess's posture tells me that what we learn here is going to be a bit stilted. Not false but sterile.

The veil says our Fool isn't going to get the whole picture. What he gets is important. He can't go further without learning about Boaz and Jachin, but it's book learning. It's a partial reflection of the truth.

Behind our view is something tantalizing, maybe even deadly. We don't know if the priestess is hiding a sandy beach or a tsunami.

To the Christian, the Bible plays the important role of The Priestess. It is the book that reflects everything we're supposed to know about God. I have never heard anybody suggest that it contains absolutely everything about God because parts are beyond our grasp. They say that what's revealed is all we need to know to get us cleared for landing in heaven, but they'll admit there's more to God than can be expressed in ink.

God's totality is hidden behind a veil. Yes, the Christ split the veil for us, but I believe my head would explode (or implode) if I had to take in God's totality all at once.

Book learning has problems. Some say we have to take the Good Book in its totality. That means women are the property of men. Sinners ought to be killed. Animals are to be sacrificed.

Figure 5: Lev. 11:9-12

A better attitude might be that some parts of the bible are inspired or currently applicable. If that's true, we have to be able to tell which are the sections we can jettison. Some say that being gay is an abomination, an idea from the pages of Leviticus. That's the same book that says bats are birds. Women who give birth to a boy are "unclean" for a week. If it's a baby girl, mama is unclean for two weeks. The cure for leprosy includes rubbing oil into the leper's right ear and right thumb.

The author of a large part of the Christian Bible — Saint Paul — was critical of the scribes who copied Paul's letters for distribution. He didn't like all the mistakes the scribes made. So if the Bible is letter-for-letter the Word of God, did He sanction all the human errors in getting His Word to our generation?

> All who rely on observing the law are under a curse, for it is written: "Cursed is everyone who does not continue to do everything written in the Book of the Law." [Galatians 3:10]

There's nothing wrong with book-learning. It is definitely a good *starting point* for many adventures, but the reflection of a truth isn't the truth itself.

Hotei – the laughing Buddha – taught that when the Master points to the moon, some students think the finger is the moon.

Mark Twain said there are two kinds of education. The first kind is reading about carrying a cat home by the tail. The second kind of education will give you lessons that are unlikely to grow dim with time.

Figure 6: Hotei

> But, on the other hand, Uncle Abner said that the person that had took a bull by the tail once had learnt sixty or seventy times as much as a person that hadn't, and said a person that started in to carry a cat home by the tail was gitting knowledge that was always going to be useful to him, and warn't ever going to grow dim or doubtful. [Mark Twain, *Tom Sawyer Abroad*]

The Priestess is the reflection of truth, and her lessons are more valuable when we remember their limitations. If the lessons learned here are muddled, just wait. Other cards will slap you around until you absorb and assimilate each lesson.

In my opinion, this is the great danger with Evangelical Christian groups. They are *solo scriptura*.[11] Words are just ink spots on paper. Some ink spots can be beautiful, others profound. A few are important. But they are still just splotches of ink that may or may not convey a meaning. We hope that the meaning is what God would want us to receive, not marred by the subjective view of the author or the imperfect ability of the scribes and translators.

Mistakes as harmless as a comma can create a mess:

a) Let's go eat, granny.
b) Let's go eat granny.

If you take the greatest Bible verse (pick one) and compare it to God, God wins. The verse won't even make a decent showing in the contest. Some of those fundamentalist groups allow their adherents to stop spiritual growth at The Priestess, and that's just a reflection of the bounty in store for the rest of us.

I know Bible-oriented Christians who don't mistake the pointing finger for the moon, but it seems like *sola scriptura* folks are led right up to the edge of an over-simplified reality map.

Back at the first card, our Fool was on an edge. Hopefully it isn't the *sola scriptura* precipice that is devoid of the patina earned by a life lived thoroughly and right on the edge, a life of triumphs and stumbles.

---

[11] "through scripture alone"

A. E. WAITE'S NOTES ON THE PRIESTESS

*She has the lunar crescent at her feet, a horned diadem on her head, with
a globe in the middle place, and a large solar cross on her breast. The scroll
in her hands is inscribed with the word Tora, signifying the Greater Law, the
Secret Law and the second sense of the Word. It is partly covered by her
mantle, to shew that some things are implied and some spoken. She is
seated between the white and black pillars — J. and B. — of the mystic
Temple, and the veil of the Temple is behind her: it is embroidered with
palms and pomegranates. The vestments are flowing and gauzy, and the
mantle suggests light — a shimmering radiance. She has been called occult
Science on the threshold of the Sanctuary of Isis, but she is really the Secret
Church, the House which is of God and man. She represents also the Second Marriage of the Prince who is no longer of this world; she is the spiritual Bride and Mother, the daughter of the stars and the Higher Garden of
Eden. She is, in fine, the Queen of the borrowed light, but this is the light of
all. She is the Moon nourished by the milk of the Supernal Mother.*

*In a manner, she is also the Supernal Mother herself — that is to say, she
is the bright reflection. It is in this sense of reflection that her truest and
highest name in Kabala is Shekinah[12] — the co-habiting glory. According to
Kabalism,[13] there is a Shekinah both above and below. In the superior
world it is called Binah, the Supernal Understanding which reflects to the
emanations that are beneath. In the lower world it is Malkuth — that
world being, for this purpose, understood as a blessed Kingdom that with
which it is made blessed being the Indwelling Glory. Mystically speaking, the
Shekinah is the Spiritual Bride of the just man, and when he reads the Law
she gives the Divine meaning. There are some respects in which this card is
the highest and holiest of the Greater Arcana.*

---

[12] A Hebrew word (feminine) for the divine presence or holy light.

[13] A mystical tradition in Judaism. The word refers to the reception of a verbal
or secret teaching.

Card 3. The Empress

> To every thing there is a season, and a time to every purpose under the heaven.
> [Turn, Turn, Turn — Ecclesiastes 3 (as told to Pete Seeger)]

If The Priestess was puckered and prim, The Empress is just a regular gal. The Fool's previous stop was with a reflection that had unnecessarily perfect posture. The Empress: not so much. She's almost lounging on her chair. She has pillows with lumbar support.

On the ground is something that looks like a heart-shaped box of chocolates. It's actually a shield, festooned with the symbol of Venus.

The Empress is sporting a very nice crown of stars, and that's supposed to invoke the idea that she's the queen of heaven. Isis has been regarded as the queen of heaven for thousands of years. She was the only one venerated everywhere in ancient Egypt. Every town had its own set of goddesses, but Isis was on the list everywhere.

Isis married her brother, Osiris. If that raised eyebrows, I haven't seen the reports. She didn't seem to care. They were husband/wife and brother/sister.

Hubby was killed by Set, another brother. The story was that the yearly flood of the Nile River was actually caused by the tears of Isis. She never sat still over this. Set had dissected Osiris's body, and Isis ran around the countryside collecting body pieces. She got almost everything and brought Osiris back to life.

This is where the story turns from strange to haunting and icky. A fish chewed up and swallowed Osiris's penis, so Isis made him a new one and somehow glued it to the now-resurrected body.[14]

The pomegranate is a symbol of fertility. We first saw pomegranates on The Priestess card, but they were detached from the main fig-

---

[14] Religion studies for the youngsters of ancient Egypt must have been oodles more colorful than the ones I attended in Texas.

ure. We had the fruit hiding some kind of water (ocean, beach, or possibly a tsunami).

The pomegranates get a makeover here. Our empress has them on her on her robe. They hide her body but are far from detached. The fertility of these pomegranates is right up against the skin of The Empress.

There's no longer a veil hiding the action of some kind of mysterious water. The flow of water that began with the gown of the priestess has become a waterfall on The Empress, and there's nothing hidden about it. Fertility is front and center.

The Empress is holding an orb, a symbol of royalty. In other tarot decks, she also holds a scepter. Waite and Smith combined those separate objects into one. Our empress has her orb on the end of a stick. Maybe it's a double dose of her brand of authority.

What I notice when I see her holding up this org/scepter is that she almost looks like she's offering a toast to us.

"Salud," I can hear her say as she wishes us health.

As the Fool sashays up to raise his own orb or goblet to meet hers, he has to cross a field. That's wheat growing at the bottom of the card. It isn't ready to be used for flour yet because the wheat is still growing.

> *Now there were certain Greeks among those who came up to worship at the feast. Then they came to Philip, who was from Bethsaida of Galilee, and asked him, saying, "Sir, we wish to see Jesus." Philip came and told Andrew, and in turn Andrew and Philip told Jesus.*
>
> *But Jesus answered them, saying, "The hour has come that the Son of Man should be glorified. Most assuredly, I say to you, unless a grain of wheat falls into the ground and dies, it remains alone; but if it dies, it produces much grain. He who loves his life will lose it, and he who hates his life in this world will keep it for eternal life. If anyone serves Me, let him follow Me; and where I am, there My servant will be also. If anyone serves Me, him My Father will honor.*
>
> [John 12:20-26]

Jesus was talking about himself in this passage, said to be from late in His earthly ministry. Like the grains of wheat, we know that Jesus had to die on the cross before the resurrection could be possible. Osiris had to be killed and dismembered before Isis could use her intense struggle and sorcery to paste him back together.

The Fool faces all kinds of contradictions.

- The Empress is in a gown showing pomegranates, stressing fertility because each fruit contains so many seeds.
- We have a waterfall of emotions flowing toward the field of wheat.
- Waters of life come to nourish the golden stalks, even though we know that each grain must die before it can give us nourishment.
- The Fool sees that the lady is relaxed and inviting. Isis was an empress with a rough edge, especially if you kidnapped and dismembered her husband.

The empress is comfortable on her cushions. Wearing that crown of heavenly authority doesn't seem to weigh her down.

What we have here is a spiritual guide. She seems relaxed, maybe a bit worldly. She doesn't hide possible troubles (waterfalls can be deadly). If you know anything about crops, you know that the wheat between you and the Empress is ready to die. But death and change are all aspects of life, and the Empress is telling us to embrace both sides of that coin.

And if The Fool has a take-away from this stop on his adventure, it's to learn by imitation. We don't have to sugarcoat anything for anyone, but we should always be ready to seem inviting. We have to walk with our brothers and sisters, regardless of their path or circumstance.

Do not let your hearts be troubled. You believe in and adhere to and trust in and rely on God; believe in and adhere to and trust in and rely also on Me. [John 14:1]

> Carry one another's burdens and troublesome moral faults, and in this way fulfill and observe perfectly the law of Christ.
>
> [Galatians 6: 2]

> Not like the brazen giant of Greek fame,
>
> With conquering limbs astride from land to land;
>
> Here at our sea-washed, sunset gates shall stand
>
> A mighty woman with a torch, whose flame
>
> Is the imprisoned lightning, and her name
>
> Mother of Exiles. From her beacon-hand
>
> Glows world-wide welcome; her mild eyes command
>
> The air-bridged harbor that twin cities frame.
>
> "Keep, ancient lands, your storied pomp!" cries she
>
> With silent lips. **"Give me your tired, your poor,**
>
> **Your huddled masses yearning to breathe free**,
>
> The wretched refuse of your teeming shore.
>
> Send these, the homeless, tempest-tost to me,
>
> I lift my lamp beside the golden door!"
>
> ["The New Colossus" (sonnet), Emma Lazarus (1849-1887)]

A. E. WAITE'S NOTES ON THE EMPRESS

A stately figure, seated, having rich vestments and royal aspect, as of a daughter of heaven and earth. Her diadem is of twelve stars, gathered in a cluster. The symbol of Venus is on the shield which rests near her. A field of corn is ripening in front of her, and beyond there is a fall of water. The sceptre which she bears is surmounted by the globe of this world. She is the inferior Garden of Eden, the Earthly Paradise, all that is symbolized by the visible house of man. She is not Regina coeli,[15] but she is still refugium peccatorum,[16] the fruitful mother of thousands. There are also certain aspects in which she has been correctly described as desire and the wings thereof, as the woman clothed with the sun, as Gloria Mundi[17] and the veil of the Sanctum Sanctorum[18] but she is not, I may add, the soul that has attained wings, unless all the symbolism is counted up another and unusual way. She is above all things universal fecundity and the outer sense of the Word. This is obvious, because there is no direct message, which has been given to man like that which is borne by woman; but she does not herself carry its interpretation.

In another order of ideas, the card of the Empress signifies the door or gate by which an entrance is obtained into this life, as into the Garden of Venus; and then the way which leads out therefrom, into that which is beyond, is the secret known to the High Priestess: it is communicated by her to the elect. Most old attributions of this card are completely wrong on the symbolism — as, for example, its identification with the Word, Divine Nature, the Triad, and so forth.

---

[15] queen of heaven

[16] safe haven of sinners

[17] glory of the world

[18] holy of holies *[See, mama! All those years studying Latin finally paid off. I didn't have to look up any of this stuff.]*

Card 4. The Emperor

> *"Experience is a good school but the fees are high."*
>
> [Heinrich Heine (1797-1856)]

When our traveling Fool encounters The Emperor, the wanderer knows that he's in the presence of somebody who's been around the block. You don't grow a beard that long in an afternoon.

This is tarot's father figure. We're back to a stone throne, so comfort isn't at play here. The emperor's legs are under armor, telling us he's seen battle.

He is going to be setting down the law and will demand we listen. The priestess wanted to tell us things, too, but everything was the reflection of something else. This emperor is full of personal experience. He's knows what he knows, and expects compliance.

The throne has ram heads on the arms and back. They symbolize action. Aries.

Off in the background, we can see the waters are still flowing, but the emperor commands our attention here.

Alcoholic Anonymous stresses examples that come from personal experience. Members say that opinions are like smelly butts: everybody has them but they are only good for getting rid of stuff. They downplay book learning in favor of personal experience. Recovery in AA comes in the form of the lessons of what has worked for others. That's what The Emperor offers. He's crusty. He's opinionated. He probably hasn't any patience for the naïve or the whiner. The main thing he shows us is a life lived. He has been an active participant of his own life, and that's his biggest lesson. Life consists of effort.

He has an orb in one hand and a staff in the other.

The emperor's staff is really an ankh, and that's the most critical element of the picture. The ancients in Egypt taught their children that the gods and goddesses needed help to keep things going.

A symbol of life was the sun. At sunset, the gods of the under-world pushed the sun along, keeping it safe until they could push it back up on the other side of the world at sunrise. It was in their care, so to speak.

At sunrise, the gods and goddesses of the day would push the sun across the sky to keep it moving. That's summarized in a symbol that appears over and over in ancient Egypt, the scarab or dung beetle. In reality, those insects collect poop in little balls and roll them around, but it looked like something pushing the sun.

Figure 7: scarab beetle

Figure 8: drywall hawk

The point is that keeping the sun moving takes effort, and the gods/goddesses need our help.

The ankh is like a drywall hawk, the handheld tool that lets drywall or plaster craftsmen carry mortar or plaster. When you see the ankh — whether in the hand of The Emperor or elsewhere — remember that it shows the gods/goddesses need our efforts.

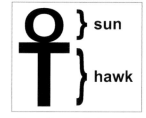

Figure 9: ankh "schematic"

> Narrow is the road that leads to the life of a violinist. Hour after hour, day after day and week after week, for years, I lived with my violin. There were so many things that I wanted to do that I had to leave undone; there were so many places I wanted to go that I had to miss if I was to master the violin. The road that I traveled was a narrow road and the way was hard.
>
> [Fritz Kreisler, violinist (1875-1962)]

A. E. WAITE'S NOTES ON THE EMPEROR

> He has a form of the Crux ansata[19] for his sceptre and a globe in his left hand. He is a crowned monarch — commanding, stately, seated on a throne, the arms of which axe fronted by rams' heads. He is executive and realization, the power of this world, here clothed with the highest of its natural attributes. He is occasionally represented as seated on a cubic stone, which, however, confuses some of the issues. He is the virile power, to which the Empress responds, and in this sense is he who seeks to remove the Veil of Isis;[20] yet she remains virgo intacta.[21]
>
> It should be understood that this card and that of the Empress do not precisely represent the condition of married life, though this state is implied. On the surface, as I have indicated, they stand for mundane royalty, uplifted on the seats of the mighty; but above this there is the suggestion of another presence. They signify also — and the male figure especially — the higher kingship, occupying the intellectual throne. Hereof is the lordship of thought rather than of the animal world. Both personalities, after their own manner, are "full of strange experience," but theirs is not consciously the wisdom, which draws from a higher world. The Emperor has been described as
>
> a) will in its embodied form, but this is only one of its applications, and
>
> b) as an expression of virtualities contained in the Absolute Being — but this is fantasy.

---

[19] handled cross. It is sometimes an ankh. Crux Ansata was also the title of a book by H. G. Wells that attacked the Vatican for its behavior during World War Two. The H. G. Wells book came along about forty years after these notes from A. E. Waite. Yes, Wells and Waite knew each other. No, I don't know if the title of the Wells book had anything to do with Waite's notes on tarot. (sorry... hanging head in shame)

[20] "I am all that hath been, and is, and shall be; and my veil no mortal has hitherto raised." Plutarch (46-120AD) says this inscription about the Veil of Isis was in stone at a Shrine of Isis at Sais in the Nile delta of ancient Egypt. Priests in Egypt would perform a ceremonial parting of the goddess's veil during liturgies and restore it at the rite's close.

[21] Waite's just showing off now. The phrase just means an "intact virgin." Yes, others have used the term, but it's still a bit redundant. An intact virgin is like an unmarried bachelor. Saying somebody's a bachelor sort of includes the notion of unmarried. Just sayin'—.

Card 5. The Hierophant

Our poor Fool next lands for a session with the Hierophant, and he is in for the shock of his tender, young life.

I need to vent for a minute or two:

This is alleged to be a picture of the Pope. Both Arthur Waite and Pamela Smith were adherents of the Roman Catholic Church, so they knew what a pope is supposed to look like.

The man is wearing a triple crown, the symbol of the Papacy.

That white hanging thingy around his neck is a pallium, an adornment properly given out only to the pope's closes buddies.

In his left hand our impostor-pope is holding a ferula. That's the triple cross that identifies the bearer as the pope (if you had doubts after seeing the crown). The trouble is that the ferula is the pope's crosier, the shepherd's staff. Other bishops and archbishops carry a cross with a hook at the top end. The pope gets the ferula. Assuming the picture is accurate and the cross is resting on the person's leg, he can only walk stooped way over. The ferula is way too short, like it's a ferula-scepter or some other kind of weirdness.

His undergarment is an alb. Hidden way under that would be his cassock. The outer robe — the chasuble — means the next lower garment is an alb (ignoring the remote chance there's a hidden dalmatic in the mix). "Alb" come from the Latin word for white. Hello! An alb is white. It isn't by accident that the garment is called white. It's white! Always. No exceptions, not even for an impostor-pope. This guy is wearing a blue alb.

The pope's shoes are almost always red, unless you are a member of the Dominican Order. Red. The picture shows white slippers, and they probably even Prada brand!

I will give our poor prelate a pass on the hand signal because he's doing what's popular. We're supposed to think he's bestowing some kind of papal blessing on us, but he really looks like he's a saluting like a cub scout.

The traditional hand signal of Roman bishops (including the bishop of Rome) is a hand gesture that's a little tricky to do. It is a visual monogram of Jesus: ICXC in medieval Greek spelling. The monogram is more common among Greek and Russian Christians.

Figure 10: ICXC

You know the game called *Twister*? This is the bishop's version that he (or she) plays solitaire.

The bishop scrunches up his right hand to form all these letters at once, and then he twists his arm so we see his bishop ring. It is the ring that is doing the actual blessing, a consecrated ring with an amethyst (bishop) or sapphire (archbishop). That's the traditional stuff. Today's Roman church and most independent Catholic churches don't go to all that trouble.

Our pope has two bishops in front of him. One is wearing a silver chasuble with red roses. The other sports a blue chasuble with white lilies. The pope's chasuble is read, for martyrs or the Holy Spirit. Silver/gray just doesn't happen because the church considers silver to be a color of chaos. Plus, why would you wear silver when poor parishes all over the world are sending you gold?

The color blue happens but isn't very traditional. Some bishops allow blue on celebrations of the Blessed Virgin Mary. Even if all the colors were legitimate, all three would be wearing the same color. Rome takes their colors and vestments seriously, so you don't show up in puce paisley just because you think it's cool or because you got a good deal at the papal thrift store.

Thanks for letting me get all that off my chest. I'm better now.

So the Fool's side-trip is to see the pope in all his silly mistakes.

Our vagabond is conscientious and tries to the best he can with what he has to work with. These characters are presenting themselves as authorities on the liturgical rules and dogma, and the Fool is going to follow what they say. He is going to do what they command.

It's a kind of theological contract. The Roman church says that you don't have to understand everything. You just have to follow the rules, even when they appear to be bizarre or do-as-I-say-not-as-I-do.

To use a New Age vocabulary, the Romans command compliance. They are saying that if there's some error, they will deal with karma on your behalf.

The church is Christ's monarchy on earth. It is the outward and visible symbol of life in the Spirit.

I'm going out on a limb to say that the lack of detail in the specifics of the trappings seen on this tarot card tell us more than the obvious meaning. There are things on the card that are laughably wrong, if you know anything about church vestments and gear (and I know quite a bit about that).

In a very real sense, the Fool is being hoodwinked.

The Priestess card had visual cues. It was all about reflected truth and hidden teachings. There's no veil behind the Hierophant. We're supposed to believe that the religious leaders are showing everything. Nothing is hidden.

And the Fool wants to buy into it! He wants to suspend his belief that a pope character would be caught dead in a blue "alb" and white slippers. Egads!

> *When the student is ready, the teacher will appear.*
>
> [ancient axiom]

> *When the student is _really_ ready, the teacher disappears.*
>
> [Wynn Wagner]

There's nothing wrong with being a student. Experts never learn anything because they've closed off the learning switch in their noggin. They're experts. They think there's little they need or can learn.

That's crazy because there's always something to learn. These tarot cards continue to teach me every day. They're haunting and amazing at what they do. Sneaky little cards.

I have some smarts about church vestments and tools because that's what I used to do for a living. The characters made glaring and impossible mistakes in an area I know. It makes me suspect the cards of trying to pull the woolen mozzetta over my eyes in the areas where I'm clueless.

I'm still supposed to take lessons from these cards? That's a difficult request.

The cards say "trust me," but I want to protect the vagabond from them. The church guys are creepy idiots to me, and I want to tell the Fool to skip this Hierophant.

Run, little Fool. Run!

If the Fool listens to anything here, I know he's going to be sent incorrect information, maybe encouraged or compelled to do something dangerous or stupid.

It isn't surprising to see demagoguery coming from the Roman hierarchy, but I know it could be any religious authority. A few Muslim clerics are on a regrettable record as encouraging un-Muslim behavior. I've even heard a Buddhist leader spout my-way-or-the-highway nonsense.

So how does our innocent Fool listen and absorb the useful information. He doesn't know which parts are useful. He can't parse and filter the evil. None of us can, not with complete accuracy.

> *Beware of false prophets, which come to you in sheep's clothing, but inwardly they are ravening wolves. Ye shall know them by their fruits. Do men gather grapes of thorns, or figs of thistles? Even so every good tree bringeth forth good fruit; but a corrupt tree bringeth forth evil fruit. A good tree cannot bring forth evil fruit, neither can a corrupt tree bring forth good fruit. Every tree that bringeth not forth good fruit is hewn down, and cast into the fire. Wherefore by their fruits ye shall know them.* [Matthew 7:15-20]

A. E. WAITE'S NOTES ON THE HIEROPHANT

He wears the triple crown and is seated between two pillars, but they are not those of the Temple which is guarded by the High Priestess. In his left hand he holds a sceptre terminating in the triple cross, and with his right hand he gives the well-known ecclesiastical sign which is called that of esotericism, distinguishing between the manifest and concealed part of doctrine. It is noticeable in this connection that the High Priestess makes no sign. At his feet are the crossed keys, and two priestly ministers in albs[22] kneel before him. He has been usually called the Pope, which is a particular application of the more general office that he symbolizes. He is the ruling power of external religion, as the High Priestess is the prevailing genius of the esoteric, withdrawn power. The proper meanings of this card have suffered woeful admixture from nearly all hands. Grand Orient says truly that the Hierophant is the power of the keys, exoteric orthodox doctrine, and the outer side of the life, which leads to the doctrine; but he is certainly not the prince of occult doctrine, as another commentator has suggested.

He is rather the summa totius theologiæ,[23] when it has passed into the utmost rigidity of expression; but he symbolizes also all things that are righteous and sacred on the manifest side. As such, he is the channel of grace belonging to the world of institution as distinct from that of Nature, and he is the leader of salvation for the human race at large. He is the order and the head of the recognized hierarchy, which is the reflection of another and greater hierarchic order; but it may so happen that the pontiff forgets the significance of this his symbolic state and acts as if he contained within his proper measures all that his sign signifies or his symbol seeks to shew[24] forth. He is not, as it has been thought, philosophy — except on the theological side; he is not inspiration; and he is not religion, although he is a mode of its expression.

---

[22] *Ah-HAH!* I told you they were albs. Wait. He says they're kneeling in albs? Balderdash, Mr. Waite. They may be wearing albs, but the outer garment is what we see. The outer garment is a chasuble in both cases.

[23] This means the "highest (summit) of all theology." It is undoubtedly a shout-out to the authors of two books with similar names: Augustino Arpe (d. 704) and Thomas Aquinas (d. 1274).

[24] "Shew"? Really? You're going with "shew" here? Arthur never had to deal with the people who edit (read: terrorize) my books.

Card 6. The Lovers

It all hangs out in the Lovers card. They're nekkid as little jaybirds. We can only hope the Fool doesn't freak out with such a public display.

There's an angel figure. Some say it's Raphael, the symbol of heavenly healing.

The woman is in front of a fruit tree, and that's a big green snake slithering around the tree trunk.

The dude — unashamed about his "shortcomings" is in front of a tree of flames.

She is looking up to the angel. The angel is busy staring at her boobs. In the background, there is a single mountain.

Christians will know this is Adam and Eve. They aren't embarrassed or ashamed. It could be a lusty relationship. If they listen to Raphael, there's hope. But there's a big cloud between the angel and the couple. The snake in the fruit tree tells us the scene won't end well for the couple.

The Fool meets these guys in all their finest. You have your angel and a couple in lust/love. Even the snake appears to be smiling. You and I and the snake know where the story is going, but the couple and the Fool are clueless.

Each relationship has both love and sadness, and sometimes the two sides aren't evenly balanced. We've all known couples who "suffer" each other with one party abusive. Sometimes there's a health problem or money challenges. Even the worst relationship of all time had a few moments of love and happiness.

The other side of that is the loving couple. They seem so happy, and we celebrate with them.

But there's never been a single couple that didn't have to say goodbye eventually.

My college sweetheart was killed in a traffic accident a week after we moved in together. Some lovers die young. More and more end in divorce.

When a couple hangs on until one dies of old age, it's common for the other person to succumb to something soon after the first.

Is the Fool going to be sucked into a relationship that is built on lust rather than love? I'm going to say that it probably won't last, but I've been so wrong about couples before.

Do we tell the Fool to avoid what he sees in the card? If he falls in love, it will end with great sadness at some point. The snake may hasten the fall, but they all end.

> *This is My commandment, that you love one another, just as I have loved you.*   [John 15:12]

Some tarot decks show Adam standing between two women. My first reaction to that card was "go for it, dude." Then I noticed that one of the women was a babe and the other is an old crone. The elder woman was wise, while the younger one was smoking hot. I didn't like that version of the Lovers card after I noticed the different. It became a card of choices. Should he go for wisdom or sex? I know we're supposed to side with wisdom, but who's to say the beauty queen wouldn't eventually be wise?

> *Love is patient, love is kind, and is not jealous; love does not brag and is not arrogant, does not act unbecomingly; it does not seek its own, is not provoked, does not take into account a wrong suffered, does not rejoice in unrighteousness, but rejoices with the truth; bears all things, believes all things, hopes all things, endures all things. Love never fails; but if there are gifts of prophecy, they will be done away; if there are tongues, they will cease; if there is knowledge, it will be done away. For we know in part, and we prophesy in part; but when the perfect comes, the partial will be done away. When I was a child, I used to speak as a child, think as a child, reason as a child; when I became a man, I did away with childish things. For now we see in a mirror dimly, but then face to face; now I know in part, but then I shall know fully just as I also have been fully known. But now abide faith, hope, love, these three; but the greatest of these is love.*   [1 Corinthians 13:4-13]

When a couple comes to me to get married, they consider it a sacrament. What most don't know until I tell them is that the priest or bishop isn't the minister. Matrimony is the only sacrament where the recipient is also the actor. They marry each other, and the priest is merely the church's official witness.

That's where it gets weird when the Roman Rite "refuses to marry" a couple. Maybe one is divorced (as if no church prelate ever made a mistake). Maybe one isn't a Roman Catholic. Maybe it's two men or two women. Maybe gender fluidity is an issue.

The Roman church can't refuse to marry any couple because its priests are the witnesses. They can say that the couple can't use the church facilities. They can say that no Roman official can be the witness. Church canons can restrain their priests not to bless any non-compliant union.

In my opinion, those church groups cross the line when they tell the couple the "can't" get married. The church can say they can't marry in the church. They can forbid their ministers from taking part. But they need to stop short of saying "you can't marry." It crosses the line of civility when a religious group tries to impose its canons on non-adherents, and yet our church groups try to do this all the time.

Anybody can be married. Anybody. All you need are two individuals who make promises to each other. Their government may not recognize the union, but they're married to each other anyway. The church may disavow the union, but God sees it.

My opinion on the health of the relationship is guesswork. I've married people who had no chance of making it work. None.

"They'll break up in a month," I'd think as I told them to kiss at the end of the nuptials.

I've been pleasantly surprised by some of them. Some defy my prejudice and are long-termers. They love each other and forgive each other's faults. They take the good with the bad. They just love to show me up, don't they?

And there've been a few who were obviously in love, but fail to last a year. In other words, what I think about a particular couple doesn't seem to have anything to do with the couple.

There's a snake on The Lovers card. I'll probably warn the Fool about the snake because it's what I do. But in the end, it's up to the Fool and his lover. As a witness and observer, I have to keep my caustic opinions to myself. I need to learn to encourage the Fool and be there to support him during the inevitable trials.

A. E. WAITE'S NOTES ON THE LOVERS CARD

The sun shines in the zenith, and beneath is a great winged figure with arms extended, pouring down influences. In the foreground are two human figures, male and female, unveiled before each other, as if Adam and Eve when they first occupied the paradise of the earthly body. Behind the man is the Tree of Life, bearing twelve fruits, and the Tree of the Knowledge of Good and Evil is behind the woman; the serpent is twining round it. The figures suggest youth, virginity, innocence, and love before it is contaminated by gross material desire. This is in all simplicity the card of human love, here exhibited as part of the way, the truth and the life. It replaces, by recourse to first principles, the old card of marriage, which I have described previously, and the later follies, which depicted man between, vice and virtue. In a very high sense, the card is a mystery of the Covenant and Sabbath.

The suggestion in respect of the woman is that she signifies that attraction towards the sensitive life, which carries within it the idea of the Fall of Man, but she is rather the working of a Secret Law of Providence than a willing and conscious temptress. It is through her imputed lapse that man shall arise ultimately, and only by her can he complete himself. The card is therefore in its way another intimation concerning the great mystery of womanhood. The old meanings fall to pieces of necessity with the old pictures, but even as interpretations of the latter, some of them were of the order of commonplace and others were false in symbolism.

Card 7. The Chariot

> *Happiness is not a matter of intensity but of balance, order, rhythm*
> *and harmony.* [Thomas Merton (1915-1968)]

The Lovers told the Fool about lust and love. The Priestess and Hierophant preached about the absolute truth from God. By now, the poor fool is dizzy from all the input. The poor guy may be dazed from all the information. Maybe he wants to rest. At a minimum, the cart looks like he may be able to hitch a ride through his adventure.

Here we have a chariot, apparently made of stone. It isn't the kind of building material typically requested by your typical chariot designer. The idiot who built this one must be as dumb as a bucket of nails.

There are two sphinx characters, and they seem to be in charge of forward motion. They're both sitting and resting. Maybe they're union sphinxes and are on a break. The man in the cart doesn't seem angry they're not going anywhere. Maybe he's on a break too.

There are red splotches on each sphinx's face: somebody put lipstick on them.[25]

Maybe we're supposed to think that they are returning from some victorious campaign. Maybe the city is planning a great welcome. I don't buy it because they look like they are heading away from the castle in the background. Plus there's a river or moat around the castle, and I don't see a bridge.

The cart has a blue awning with white 6-pointed stars, but the man is standing to the front of the covered area. Confident. Forward-facing but immobile.

He wears a crown with an 8-pointed star. His shield seems to have a couple of moon phases represented.

> *The LORD is my shepherd; I shall not want. He maketh me to lie*
> *down in green pastures: he leadeth me beside the still waters. He*

---

[25] It reminds me of a phrase coined by Charles Spurgeon (1834-1892) in his book The Salt-Cellars (1887). He said, "A hog in a silk waistcoat is still a hog."

> *restoreth my soul: he leadeth me in the paths of righteousness for his name's sake. Yea, though I walk through the valley of the shadow of death, I will fear no evil: for thou art with me; thy rod and thy staff they comfort me. Thou preparest a table before me in the presence of mine enemies: thou anointest my head with oil; my cup runneth over. Surely goodness and mercy shall follow me all the days of my life: and I will dwell in the house of the LORD forever.*
>
> [Psalm 23]

Our vagabond has already encountered cocky cartoon characters. The Hierophant comes to mind. Now he comes into view of somebody who owns confidence. The two sphinxes make the matter black and white, no shade of gray. The charioteer has harnessed both the positive and negative, the Boaz (brash militarism) and Jachin (precise builder). Not only is the man in control, he has both beasts sitting with each other without distress and without visible harnesses.

And he pulls it off while sporting gauntlets that are way more frilly than they need to be! He just isn't concerned with what you think. He knows who he is, and doesn't need an imprimatur from you or the Hierophant or the Emperor or anybody else.

The two beasts look like they are turned away from each other. Slightly. They may want to go their separate ways but are behaving themselves. The man doesn't seem concerned about them because he's in charge. He knows if he lets the black and white pull against each other, nobody's going anywhere.

Compromise. Different creatures working to move in the same direction. The man confirms the dichotomy with his rigid shield that is tempered by the soft gauntlets. It's a fashion statement.

The card tells the vagabond that having a cat's attitude works to manage opposite forces into a clear direction. Cats are famous for being able to convey "I meant to do that" in most situations. They can fall because of some klutzy moment, but they always show that the fall was exactly what they intended. "Who you laughing at?"

If any piece of the picture is missing, everything stops. We need the two wheels, both sphinxes. Most of all we need the charioteer, the one who manages everything else with aplomb and understated chutzpah.

Learn confidence, little Fool. It will serve you well.

> *In the last analysis, the individual person is responsible for living his own life and for "finding himself." If he persists in shifting his responsibility to somebody else, he fails to find out the meaning of his own existence.* [Thomas Merton]

A. E. WAITE'S NOTES ON THE CHARIOT

An erect and princely figure carrying a drawn sword and corresponding, broadly speaking, to the traditional description, which I have given in the first part. On the shoulders of the victorious hero are supposed to be the Urim and Thummim.[26]

He has led captivity captive; he is conquest on all planes — in the mind, in science, in progress, in certain trials of initiation. He has thus replied to the sphinx, and it is on this account that I have accepted the variation of Éliphas Lévi; two sphinxes thus draw his chariot. He is above all things triumph in the mind.

It is to be understood for this reason—
  a) *that the question of the sphinx is concerned with a Mystery of Nature and not of the world of Grace, to which the charioteer could offer no answer;*
  b) *that the planes of his conquest are manifest or external and not within himself;*
  c) *that the liberation which he effects may leave himself in the bondage of the logical understanding;*
  d) *that the tests of initiation through which he has passed in triumph are to be understood physically or rationally; and*
  e) *that if he came to the pillars of that Temple between which the High Priestess is seated, he could not open the scroll called Tora, nor if she questioned him could he answer. He is not hereditary royalty and he is not priesthood.*

---

[26] Urim (enlightenment) and Thummim (innocence) are symbols of the breastplate on the high priests is the Jewish temple. If you have a question for the priest, you have to face the breast-plate and choose. Do you want light or truth?

Card 8. Strength

> *Always aim at complete harmony of thought and word and deed.*
> *Always aim at purifying your thoughts and everything will be well.*
> [Mahatma Gandhi (1869-1948)]

Be careful trying to talk to the Fool at this point. He's just been with the charioteer, and he's absorbed all the self-assurance that he can hold. He's cocky. He may be rude and in a mood to start a fight so he can display is new abilities. The Charioteer rubbed off, and the fool has adopted the attitude of a cat.

He is all "I meant to do that" on the outside, but a complete scaredy-cat on the inside.

He's still a simple vagabond, but there's little chance of reminding him of that. Not here. Not now.

He meets the lady called Strength on some pasture, maybe some grassland portion of Africa's Serengeti. The lady has a kitty. Here, kitty, kitty.

Can the cocky Fool ever hope to be able to pet the king of the Serengeti?

The lady is chummy with the big cat, and she is pulling it off without any force. We saw the charioteer in control of his situation, and it worked for him to do that. He needed his beasts and equipment all going the same direction. Strength doesn't seem to be trying to compel her cat to do anything. They're just hanging out. Natural enemies are spending a few moments being friendly in the grasslands.

I think the lion is picking up the love and smoothness of the lady's aura. Her energy field is telling the cat things that words can't convey. She is petting the lion, and she'd doing that with complete love and grace. She's giving the lion the honor and respect he deserves.

The woman sees a great lion. The lion must see something it likes in the woman, or he'd turn her into dim-sum without breaking a sweat.

> *Blessed are the poor in spirit: for theirs is the kingdom of heaven. Blessed are they that mourn: for they shall be comforted. Blessed are the meek: for they shall inherit the earth. Blessed are they, which do hunger and thirst after righteousness: for they shall be filled. Blessed are the merciful: for they shall obtain mercy. Blessed are the pure in heart: for they shall see God. Blessed are the peacemakers: for they shall be called the children of God. Blessed are they, which are persecuted for righteousness' sake: for theirs is the kingdom of heaven. Blessed are ye, when men shall revile you, and persecute you, and shall say all manner of evil against you falsely, for my sake.* [Matthew 5:3-11]

The confidence of a soldier has its place. The charioteer will get you from Point A to Point B.

The grace of "gentle strength" can do things that no unflappable person can hope to achieve. The charioteer came across as unshakeable in his own belief and ability. That's okay, but it definitely has limits. Ask Goliath about little David and his sling and stones. Ask George Armstrong Custer if he's still cocky after his encounter with the Lakota Sioux, Cheyenne, and Arapaho on that grassy field in Montana.

> *A gentle answer turns away wrath, but a harsh word stirs up anger.* [Proverbs 15:1]

The charioteer made a connection with the Fool. It was physical and powerful. The lady of Strength connects with the lion and hopefully with our traveler, but it isn't physical. Her "strength" isn't muscular, it's spiritual.

The lion's power (rage?) is never far from the discussion, but the woman is touching the lion. Her gentle strokes offer the lion honor. The relationship would fall apart if Strength tried to get the lion hooked up to a chariot. She would never be able to get close to the lion if she came at him like an emperor or pope. The lady shows respect and love, and I'm not sure if it is natural or just a technique. It doesn't matter because the result is the same.

The Fool's lesson here is that meek isn't weak.

A. E. WAITE'S NOTES ON THE STRENGTH CARD

A woman, over whose head there broods the same symbol of life, which we have seen in the card of the Magician, is closing the jaws of a lion. The only point in which this design differs from the conventional presentations is that her beneficent fortitude has already subdued the lion, which is being led by a chain of flowers. For reasons, which satisfy myself, this card has been interchanged with that of justice, which is usually numbered eight. As the variation carries nothing with it, which will signify to the reader, there is no cause for explanation. Fortitude, in one of its most exalted aspects, is connected with the Divine Mystery of Union; the virtue, of course, operates in all planes, and hence draws on all in its symbolism. It connects also with innocentia inviolata,[27] and with the strength, which resides in contemplation.

These higher meanings are, however, matters of inference, and I do not suggest that they are transparent on the surface of the card. They are intimated in a concealed manner by the chain of flowers, which signifies, among many other things, the sweet yoke and the light burden of Divine Law, when it has been taken into the heart of hearts. The card has nothing to do with self-confidence in the ordinary sense, though this has been suggested — but it concerns the confidence of those whose strength is God, who have found their refuge in Him. There is one aspect in which the lion signifies the passions, and she who is called Strength is the higher nature in its liberation. It has walked upon the asp and the basilisk[28] and has trodden down the lion and the dragon.

---

[27] Innocent and unviolated (or unscaled, like a mountain peak)

[28] The king of the reptiles in the lore of ancient Greece and Rome. It carried a deadly venom, but you were probably dead before it bit you because some old stories say it could kill you just by looking at you. In drawings, it usually looked like a ferret with lizard scales.

Card 9. The Hermit

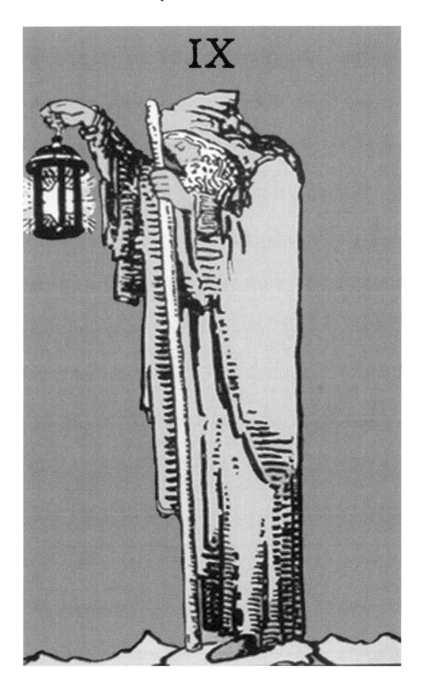

> *If you don't like what you're doing, you can always pick up your needle and move to another groove.* [Timothy Leary (1920-1996)]

Our minds wait to react until they spot a dichotomy. Most of the time we don't realize that we're submersed in earth's atmosphere. We know about the air when there's a strong wind. We really know about it when we swim underwater.

Without contrast, our hyper-developed intelligence is fairly ignorant.

We only know it is cold because we've experienced hot. If you didn't know the night, you'd never recognize the day. We live in a world of contrasts.

The Hermit reminds us to unplug from the contrasts. There's life and love that doesn't need to be separated into things we can understand. Some things just are. God doesn't have a good side or a bad side.

We have our daily grind, a "reality" that we've created for ourselves.

The relentless schedules of "I have to do this" daily life can be caustic, leaving holes in our spirits. Spiritual ulcers. Our beliefs are so dysfunctional and neurotic that our "meditation" merely makes the neurosis more efficient. Our broken philosophies become entrenched. We hold onto the good things, and that's just as damaging as holding onto the bad things.

We do something because it makes us feel good or because of our obligation to others.

We consider the lilies, and we can see their beauty and innocence and dignity. And when we really appreciate the wonderful nature of a flower, we murder it so we can stick it into a vase full of water. We want dominion over all of creation. Our admiration of things is murderous, even when we think we love and appreciate. *Run, little flowers. Run for safety.*

The Hermit stands to remind us that there are some things that have no "because" attached. We don't have to us "in order to" when we smell a rose. We can lose ourselves in a waterfall or mountain landscape without hoping to get a better job because of it.

We listen to music, and enjoying the song — every note — is the important point. We aren't trying to accomplish some final chord at the end of the song. Alan Watts said if music had a purpose, the "best" songs would be the fastest tempo because those songs would get us to their final note more urgently than a slow ballad. We don't hum a melody just so we can land on the last note! Music has no ultimate note. We enjoy the entire melody.

> *Music can be made anywhere, is invisible and does not smell.*
> [W. H. Auden (1907-1973)]

Light is a most mystical idea. It touches philosophy ("inner light" means enlightenment) and science ("speed of light" is as fast as you can get).

If you step back, you see that light is what connects us to the universe. Are we going to be able to visit distant stars? Not in our lifetime, but seeing them is a way to be there. It takes millions of years for the light of a distant start to reach the earth, and the vision is warped and distorted as it goes through our atmosphere, but we can still see the star.

> *Ye are the light of the world. A city that is set on an hill cannot be hid. Neither do men light a candle, and put it under a bushel, but on a candlestick; and it giveth light unto all that are in the house. Let your light so shine before men, that they may see your good works, and glorify your Father which is in heaven.*
> [Matthew 5:14-16]

The hermit carries a staff (walking stick) and a lamp. He's in an ankle-length hoodie (all the rage in hermit communities this year). He doesn't have baggage. We see no food or fanny pack.

The staff is masculine (phallic). It also shows the bearer is on a journey (pilgrimage). It can be a magic wand or a sign of nobility. When Moses raised his staff, it changed a whole battlefield. Lots of gods have carried staffs: Ba'al (Phoenicia), Anubis (Egypt), Hermes (Greece), Mercury (Rome).

Esoteric images use the staff to symbolize an energy flow. We saw it here, in the Magician card.

Angelina Jolie tore up a swath of bad guys in Lara Croft: Tomb Raider with her staff. And I am busy questioning myself for thinking of that right now, but it shows there's nothing sissy about a staff or walking staff. The Hermit seems so compliant and passive, but the tool he carries is far from peaceful in other stories. The Hermit's lamp is a conduit of energy that can reach out across the heavens, but he carries the phallus of spiritual energies.

But to what end? It seems like a foolish question for the Hermit. Does the Hermit have a purpose?

The Hermit speaks from the quiet interior of his heart, and he doesn't always use regular words. His "goal" is the mystical union with God (universe).

> No matter how big the call, no matter how small, you have no idea of what God is calling you to do, but God needs you. He needs me. He needs all of us.
> [St. Mychal Judge (1933-2001), his last sermon, 9/10/2001]

We can only hope the Fool sees how important it is to stay connected with the universe (light). We know he will always do best when he balances out Do and Don't Do.

At the same time, we pray our vagabond doesn't use chemicals as his body and soul cry to withdraw and regroup.

The Hermit stands alone. Withdrawn. Contemplative.

> *MY LORD GOD, I have no idea where I am going. I do not see the road ahead of me. I cannot know for certain where it will end. Nor do I really know myself, and the fact that I think that I am following your will does not mean that I am actually doing so. But I believe that the desire to please you does in fact please you. And I hope I have that desire in all that I am doing. I hope that I will never do anything apart from that desire. And I know that if I do this you will lead me by the right road though I may know nothing about it. Therefore will I trust you always though I may seem to be lost and in the shadow of death. I will not fear, for you are ever with me, and you will never leave me to face my perils alone.*

> [Thomas Merton]

A. E. WAITE'S NOTES ON THE HERMIT

The variation from the conventional models in this card is only that the lamp is not enveloped partially in the mantle of its bearer, who blends the idea of the Ancient of Days with the Light of the World It is a star which shines in the lantern. I have said that this is a card of attainment, and to extend this conception the figure is seen holding up his beacon on an eminence. Therefore the Hermit is not, as Court de Gébelin[29] explained, a wise man in search of truth and justice; nor is he, as a later explanation proposes, an especial example of experience. His beacon intimates that "where I am, you also may be."

It is further a card, which is understood quite incorrectly when it is connected with the idea of occult isolation, as the protection of personal magnetism against admixture. This is one of the frivolous renderings which we owe to Éliphas Lévi. It has been adopted by the French Order of Martinism and some of us have heard a great deal of the Silent and Unknown Philosophy enveloped by his mantle from the knowledge of the profane. In true Martinism, the significance of the term Philosophe inconnu was of another order. It did not refer to the intended concealment of the Instituted Mysteries, much less of their substitutes, but — like the card itself — to the truth that the Divine Mysteries secure their own protection from those who are unprepared.

---

[29] Born Antoine Court (1719-1784), he claimed to be a fortune teller to King Louis XVI. A chapter on tarot in *Le Monde primitif, analysé et comparé avec le monde moderne* ("The Primitive World, Analyzed and Compared to the Modern World"), 1781, became the basis of tarot readings (cartomancy) still in use today.

Card 10. Wheel of Fortune

> *God grant me the serenity to accept the things I cannot change, the courage to change the things I can, and the wisdom to know the difference. Living one day at a time; Enjoying one moment at a time; Accepting hardships as the pathway to peace; Taking, as He did, this sinful world as it is, not as I would have it; Trusting that He will make all things right if I surrender to His Will; That I may be reasonably happy in this life and supremely happy with Him Forever in the next.* [Reinhold Niebuhr (1892-1971)]

One of my fields of study in college was philosophy, and one of the hardest classes I took was ontology. That's the study of being. What exactly are you doing when you say "I am." When you say "I am" we think the meaning is obvious, but what does it really mean? What kind of activity is "I am"?

As it turns out, there's no good answer. Preachers and mystics will try to convince you otherwise, but anybody who's read Ontology will be able to knock down even the most heroic opinion.

On the first day of Ontology class, the professor asked an innocuous question: "What is life?" It wasn't a rhetorical question. The man wanted answers, and we weren't going to have any time to compose our elegant responses. He went around the class and insisted that everyone take their best shot. The room was populated by seniors and a few juniors, so this wasn't an entry-level group of people. We were experts, and we'd read plenty of monographs and other mind-numbing treatises. We were all profound in our attempt to show the man how we commanded the subject matter, even without any lessons from him.

When we were finished, he just looked at us with fingers folded under chin.

"Nope," he said after a pregnant pause. "Life is one damn thing after another."

I didn't see that coming. None of us did.

He wasn't a regular professor, so nobody really knew the man. He was basically retired from regular teaching. Ontology was his only class, and that's a shame because he was completely hysterical. Philosophy classes in the wrong hands can make you entire soul implode. Your mind is trying to figure a way to escape from your body to get some peace and quite. Relentless logic breaks apart the most beautiful topics and leaves pieces strewn all around. There are radioactive chips of dignity you have to dodge. There are scary forests of long-held truisms that you have to walk through. And you only have a silly diploma when you're done because no grocery store chain ever advertises "Wanted Philosophy Majors." You have a ton of student debt and one sheepskin.

That's what I think of when I see the Wheel of Fortune. It's the "this too will pass" card.

> *For God is not a God of disorder but of peace.*
> [1 Corinthians 14:33]

The Fool has gone from the dimness of the Hermit into the blue sky of the Wheel. A blue sphinx sits on top of the wheel, and he's holding a sword. You can think of swords as meaning "cut to the chase" when they appear on tarot cards. They are associated with the mystical element of air. They are the sharp tongue of someone who is mentally alert, possibly with an attitude.

If we were playing rock-paper-scissors, the wooden staff of the Hermit doesn't stand a chance against the sword of the blue sphinx.

> *The individual has always had to struggle to keep from being over-whelmed by the tribe. If you try it, you will be lonely often, and sometimes frightened. But no price is too high to pay for the privilege of owning yourself.* [Friedrich Nietzsche (1844-1900)]

As the wheel spins, it spells out T-A-R-O and loops back for the final T.

The poor Fool is assaulted by images. Clockwise from the blue sphinx comes a naked man with some kind of animal head, possibly a wolf. A yellow or golden snake follows next. In the four corners are the symbols of the four "fixed" astrological signs:

- eagle (scorpio in some explanations),
- bull (taurus),
- lion (leo), and
- angel (aquarius).

I can imagine the Fool getting confused. He was presented with the four mystical elements way back at the Magician. Now he has Hebrew letters on a wheel that's spinning around creepy characters, and four zodiac thingies are looking on.

"Dude," he says. "Pick a lane!"

> *Everyone thinks of changing the world, but no one thinks of changing himself.*
> [Leo Tolstoy (1828-1910)]

The Wheel card symbolizes life's "rat race." If something bad is happening, we know it will get better. When it gets better, do we cling to that? Of course we cling to the good, even though that leads us to desperation and psychiatrists and their antidepressants.

Ontology for most of us is collecting toys. We build the nest egg that the experts say we have to have. They're right, of course, but it doesn't mean we should put blinders on our eyes. It doesn't mean we can't unplug from time to time. We can be the hermit, sitting beside a great waterfall with its crashing sounds of emotion.

What's missing from the Waite-Smith depiction of the hermit is that he's standing at a front door. He's about to knock. He's about to remind us what "I am" really means on a deep and cosmic level. He's got the lantern with the light energy that connects us to the entire universe.

The hermit is about to knock on our door.

> *Conscience does make cowards of us all.*
> [William Shakespeare, Hamlet]

A. E. Waite's Notes on the Wheel of Fortune

In this symbol I have again followed the reconstruction of Éliphas Lévi, who has furnished several variants. It is legitimate — as I have intimated — to use Egyptian symbolism when this serves our purpose, provided that no theory of origin is implied therein. I have, however, presented Typhon in his serpent form. The symbolism is, of course, not exclusively Egyptian, as the four Living Creatures of Ezekiel occupy the angles of the card, and the wheel itself follows other indications of Lévi in respect of Ezekiel's

Figure 11: *Éliphas Lévi (1810-1875)*

vision, as illustrative of the particular Tarot Key. With the French occultist, and in the design itself, the symbolic picture stands for the perpetual motion of a fluidic universe and for the flux of human life. The Sphinx is the equilibrium therein. The transliteration of Taro as Rota is inscribed on the wheel, counterchanged with the letters of the Divine Name — to shew that Providence is imphed[30] through all. But this is the Divine intention within, and the similar intention without is exemplified by the four Living Creatures. Sometimes the sphinx is represented couchant on a pedestal above, which defrauds the symbolism by stultifying the essential idea of stability amidst movement.

Behind the general notion expressed in the symbol there lies the denial of chance and the fatality, which is implied therein. It may be added that, from the days of Lévi onward, the occult explanations of this card are — even for occultism itself — of a singularly fatuous kind. It has been said to mean principle, fecundity, virile honour, ruling authority, etc. The findings of common fortune telling are better than this on their own plane.

---

[30] assumed, infused, or assimilated

Card 11. Justice

> *Hell is full of good meanings, but heaven is full of good works.*
> [Bernard of Clairvaux, Samuel Johnson, Billy Joel, Sir Walter
> Scott, Søren Kierkegaard, and Karl Marx, and every other deep-
> thinking writer worth a hill of beans]

The Fool was screaming "pick a lane" with the Wheel of Fortune as he was assaulted with every esoteric image that Miss Smith and Arthur Waite could think of. This card — Justice — is where that lane gets picked.

Pixie Smith apparently had a thing about uncomfortable chairs made out of stone because she drew another for Justice to use. This can't be good! You always want the person meeting out justice to be comfortable. A bad chair for the judge will probably increase his or her life sentences.

Justice is the halfway point in the Fool's adventure. The figure is most likely a woman, although there's enough ambiguity to leave that open for discussion.

There are two columns, like the Priestess and the Hierophant. There's a veil, like the Priestess, but this one is red. Red is the color of passion. If we have emotions, we're supposed to leave them hidden behind the veil while we visit Justice.

A sword in her (his) right hand signals that Justice will cut through whatever crap we bring. The blade of the sword is blue, the color of flowing emotions. The sword is a symbol of air, but this one is fashioned to cut through emotions.

> *There hath no temptation taken you but such as is common to*
> *man: but God is faithful, who will not suffer you to be tempted*
> *above that ye are able; but will with the temptation also make a*
> *way to escape, that ye may be able to bear it.*
> [1 Corinthians 10:13]

The scales in the left hand are balanced. Balanced reason. No argument based on passion will be tolerated here. Justice is going to act with a cool head (not to mention a cool and possibly sore butt, considering the chair).

There's a crown on Justice's head, and it looks like the dentils at the top of a castle. The judge's mind is a fortress, and we have no chance of using a emotional plea for mercy.

> Then the Lord said to him, "Now you Pharisees make the outside of the cup and dish clean, but your inward part is full of greed and wickedness. Foolish ones! Did not He who made the outside make the inside also? But rather give alms of such things as you have; then indeed all things are clean to you. "But woe to you Pharisees! For you tithe mint and rue and all manner of herbs, and pass by justice and the love of God. These you ought to have done, without leaving the others undone. [Luke 11:39-42]

Our vagabond — if he's like the rest of us — will go through a spell where he sits on that uncomfortable stone chair. He becomes Justice, and may not realize why that's so poisonous a thing to do.

When someone does something, we react. Sometimes we condemn. Occasionally we try to do revenge. We boil over with resentment.

I'm going to use some New Age terms to explain this. Karma. The Lords of Karma are out there bundling up a bunch of acid to send down to the person who wronged us. The moment we react strongly, we are telling those Lords not to do whatever they were planning to do.

"You mealy-mouthed creep," we tell our offender.

"Ah-hah," say the Lords of Karma. "He's going to be doing the retribution on our behalf."

The Lords are happy because they can go on a break. Drink some tea or coffee or whatever they do.

Before the Lords of Karma check out of the situation, they pile up whatever they were going to dish out to our perp and send it to us. We announced that we are dealing with the situation, so we get all the bad karma to do with as we said we'd do.

In effect, we get something like triple the badness just for thinking about revenge. If we slap the offending person, we get the bad karma for the slap. Plus we get all the slapper's original bad karma because we're doing what the Lords of Karma would otherwise have done. And then the universe doubles everything because we're supposed to know better.

> *Judge not, that ye be not judged.*[31] *For with what judgment ye judge, ye shall be judged: and with what measure ye mete, it shall be measured to you again. And why beholdest thou the mote that is in thy brother's eye, but considerest not the beam that is in thine own eye? Or how wilt thou say to thy brother, Let me pull out the mote out of thine eye; and, behold, a beam is in thine own eye? Thou hypocrite, first cast out the beam out of thine own eye; and then shalt thou see clearly to cast out the mote out of thy brother's eye. Give not that which is holy unto the dogs, neither cast ye your pearls before swine, lest they trample them under their feet, and turn again and rend you. Ask, and it shall be given you; seek, and ye shall find; knock, and it shall be opened unto you: For every one that asketh receiveth; and he that seeketh findeth; and to him that knocketh it shall be opened. Or what man is there of you, whom if his son ask bread, will he give him a stone? Or if he ask a fish, will he give him a serpent? If ye then, being evil, know how to give good gifts unto your children, how much more shall your Father which is in heaven give good things to them that ask him? Therefore all things whatsoever ye would that men should do to you, do ye even so to them: for this is the law and the prophets.*
>
> [Matthew 7:1-12]

There was a prayer written by an anonymous French soldier in World War One that is incorrectly credited to St. Francis of Assisi.

---

[31] It's like telling the Lords of Karma to stand down. "I got this one, Lords of Karma." They dutifully abandon keeping things in balance because you promised to take care of it. Instead of whoever-it-is getting their just desserts, those Lords give you all his/her karma on top of whatever you earn for yourself on the transaction. It's a double dose you really don't have to accept if you just forgive and forget and move on.

The soldier knew about karma and suffering, and he prayed for a way to neutralize all the animosity. It's easy to understand and difficult to do. I like to think of the "Peace Prayer" as a kind of <u>magical</u> formula.

> *Lord, make me an instrument of your peace.*
>
> *Where there is hatred, let me sow love.*
>
> *Where there is injury, pardon.*
>
> *Where there is doubt, faith.*
>
> *Where there is despair, hope.*
>
> *Where there is darkness, light.*
>
> *Where there is sadness, joy.*
>
> *O Divine Master,*
>
> *grant that I may not so much seek to be consoled, as to console;*
>
> *to be understood, as to understand;*
>
> *to be loved, as to love.*
>
> *For it is in giving that we receive.*
>
> *It is in pardoning that we are pardoned,*
>
> *and it is in dying that we are born to Eternal Life.*
>
> [anonymous French soldier, World War One]

To tell the universe that you want to be loved, get busy loving everyone. If you need comfort, go visit somebody who has lost a loved one. This is a cunning and very effective formula, and the universe understands it every time.

Creation isn't out to "get you." Sorry, you're just not that important in the overall cosmic experience. God loves you. Your guardian angel mostly loves you, when it isn't busy laughing at your creepy foibles.

The Lords of Karma, on the other hand, are just there to keep things in balance. They represent the scales of justice.

"Turning the other cheek" isn't a sign of weakness here. It's a magic formula that tells the Lords of Karma that they are in charge of keeping the universe balanced. It means you are willing to let them do their job. They're very good at what they do. If you screwed up, forgive somebody who wronged you. If you want some goodie or play-pretty, give something to someone else.

If you want a soothing embrace from Justice (the Lords of Karma), you will be disappointed here. Justice is about balance, no matter how uncomfortable that is. It is about finding that quiet place in the face of hatred, homophobia, injustice, fakery, bigotry, and abuse. It is about letting the Lords of Karma do what they're paid to do.

Justice isn't fun. Justice is wise. If you want fun, go watch a sitcom.

A. E. WAITE'S NOTES ON THE JUSTICE CARD

As this card follows the traditional symbolism and carries above all its obvious meanings, there is little to say regarding it outside the few considerations collected in the first part, to which the reader is referred.

It will be seen, however, that the figure is seated between pillars, like the High Priestess, and on this account it seems desirable to indicate that the moral principle which deals unto every man according to his works — while, of course, it is in strict analogy with higher things; — differs in its essence from the spiritual justice which is involved in the idea of election. The latter belongs to a mysterious order of Providence, in virtue of which it is possible for certain men to conceive the idea of dedication to the highest things. The operation of this is like the breathing of the Spirit where it wills, and we have no canon of criticism or ground of explanation concerning it. It is analogous to the possession of the fairy gifts and the high gifts and the gracious gifts of the poet: we have them or have not, and their presence is as much a mystery as their absence. The law of Justice is not however involved by either alternative. In conclusion, the pillars of Justice open into one world and the pillars of the High Priestess into another.

Card 12. Hanged Man

> *And when he had called the people unto him with his disciples also, he said unto them, Whosoever will come after me, let him deny himself, and take up his cross, and follow me. For whosoever will save his life shall lose it; but whosoever shall lose his life for my sake and the gospel's, the same shall save it.*   [Mark 8:34-35]

Tarot cards are never what they seem. The previous card — Justice — seemed like a nice card on the surface, but it is cold and uncomfortable. The Wheel of Fortune doesn't scare anybody until they look at it for more than five minutes.

The Hanged Man is one of those cards that make people cringe. Death, Devil, and the Tower are some of the others.

The man isn't showing pain. In fact, he's glowing like the sun. Only one ankle is restrained, and that does a lot less physical damage than a noose around the neck.

If you turn the card upside-down, the man is in the form of a big "4".

He's got a blue (emotions) peasant shirt and red (force) tights. Are those ballet slippers on his feet? His hair falls straight to the earth, but that's the hairdo popular with some hip young men these days. Maybe he just washed his hair, and he's letting it dry in place naturally.

Whatever he's doing, he isn't objecting to it. Maybe he's just kinky and is into some kind of self-bondage.

The scaffold appears to be wooden with a vine of some sort. The shape is an uppercase "T," which is the Tau Cross[32] that is associated with St. Francis of Assisi.

---

[32] "Tau" is how they say "T" in Greece. The cross itself has been around since the time of the pharaohs in ancient Egypt. Romans used it as a symbol of their god, Mithras. Manly P Hall says that priests placed a tau cross on the lips of a new pharaoh as they were initiated into the mysteries of the Egyptian religion [Manly P. Hall, *The Secret Teachings of All Ages*]

The man is in a position to absorb the universe, albeit topsy-turvy. It's the position most of us were in when we were born. He's tied to the tree by some kind of umbilical cord.

Odin is a Norse god, a high-ranking one. To make sure he got everything right, Odin volunteered to be hung from the Yggdrasill, an enormous tree. It is the tree that connects earth (roots) to heaven (leaves). Odin wanted to be hung on the tree so he could understand his kingdom.

> I know that I hung on a windy tree nine long nights, wounded with a spear, dedicated to Odin, myself to myself, on that tree of which no man knows from where its roots run. [Hávamál]

The Hanged Man is still in the womb. He is absorbing the universe from the point of view of an infant about to be born. Above all, the Hanged Man has volunteered for this duty. He's like Odin, who agreed to be hung from that Norse tree with the awful name (Yggdrasill). Maybe Odin was suspended until he could remember how to spell the tree's name.

> And they that are Christ's have crucified the flesh with the affections and lusts. [Galatians 5:24]

Our vagabond, inverted, agrees to be vulnerable.

"How bad do you want this enlightenment?" the universe asks. The response is the Hanged Man.

"Whatever it takes," he says.

> We thought we could find an easier, softer way. But we could not. With all the earnestness at our command, we beg of you to be fearless and thorough from the very start. Some of us have tried to hold on to our old ideas and the result was nil until we let go absolutely. ["How It Works", Alcoholics Anonymous]

What if God asked me to abandon all hope of heaven? Am I willing to do absolutely anything?

What if God told me that He wanted me to stop obsessing over that perfectly cooked ribeye steak? Is that too much to ask?

The food I most despise is the cucumber. Ick! What if I learned that the only thing that pleased God was me eating cucumbers? God forbid, but it's possible. Theoretically possible. If I didn't go hurl myself off a mountain, could I stomach a lifetime of cucumbers?

If God really is all-powerful, then He can come up with things I can't even imagine. Am I willing to buy into that? The unknown. "Ay, there's the rub," Shakespeare wrote.

Nobody said this stuff was easy.

A. E. WAITE'S NOTES ON THE HANGED MAN

The gallows from which he is suspended forms a Tau cross, while the figure — from the position of the legs — forms a fylfot[33] cross. There is a nimbus about the head of the seeming martyr. It should be noted —

1. *that the tree of sacrifice is living wood, with leaves thereon;*

2. *that the face expresses deep entrancement, not suffering;*

3. *that the figure, as a whole, suggests life in suspension, but life and not death.*

It is a card of profound significance, but all the significance is veiled. One of his editors suggests that Éliphas Lévi did not know the meaning, which is unquestionable nor did the editor himself. It has been called falsely a card of martyrdom, a card of prudence, a card of the Great Work, a card of duty; but we may exhaust all published interpretations and find only vanity. I will say very simply on my own part that it expresses the relation, in one of its aspects, between the Divine and the Universe.

He who can understand that the story of his higher nature is imbedded in this symbolism will receive intimations concerning a great awakening that is possible, and will know that after the sacred Mystery of Death there is a glorious Mystery of Resurrection.

---

[33] stylized swastika used in heraldry. It's what Waite said. I've never seen this fylfot cross peering from the Hanged Man. If you do: congrats.

Card 13. Death

> *Jesus said unto her, I am the resurrection, and the life: he that be-*
> *lieveth in me, though he were dead, yet shall he live: And whosoever*
> *liveth and believeth in me shall never die. Believest thou this?*
>
> [John 11:25-26]

The Fool is still dizzy from hanging upside down in that tree. His ankle is chafed from the robe, and he could use a break. Does tarot give him any slack? No. Is there downtime to let the brain stop spinning? Yeah, right.

Death is one of those cards that scares the little kiddies.

In the Hanged Man, the traveler said "whatever it takes." The Death card tests that bravado. Religion spins dying with stories about an afterlife, but no religion has ever been able to give verifiable proof that stands up to science. That doesn't mean religion is wrong! It just means that life after death is a matter of beliefs. Faith.

People tend not to come back after they're dead. There are "near death" experiences. We have plenty of returning people who have come back in the pages of religious texts. Jesus is an obvious example, but there are others: Ba'al, Osiris, Adonis, Melqart. Elisha in the Jewish part of the Bible raised a boy.[34]

> *It is in dying that we are born to Eternal Life.*
>
> ["Peace Prayer," anonymous]

Tarot's Death creature is a skeleton riding a white horse. The horizon has two columns, proving that Pixie Smith was obsessed with pairs of columns.

The sky is gray with the sun partially visible on the horizon. I think we're supposed to think it's sunset, but I'm not convinced. I think it may be the dawn of something new.

---

[34] 2 Kings 4

It's all so confusing with broken images everywhere. It's a mixed up at the book of Revelations in the Bible.

The skeleton is carrying a black flag with a white flower. It's probably a white rose, and maybe the rider is heading to somebody's grave. White roses and graves go with each other.

Death is staring out from the card. He seems to be looking at my right shoulder. If he'd paid more attention to his ride, he might have spared the pope who's just been trampled. We know it's the pope because of the red slippers and the winter mozzetta with its ermine fur. This is the real pope, not the impostor we found in the Hierophant card.

Arthur Waite claims the dead guy is a king. That would symbolize outward authority. He's definitely dressed like the pope, which would involve inward authority. I think it's a case for inclusivity or misdirection.

Standing in front of the horse is another Roman cleric. The headgear says he's at least a bishop, maybe an archbishop. The guy is praying. Is it a "please don't trample me" prayer, or is he praying for the repose of the dead pope's soul?

A woman in the foreground looks like she just stepped out of an over-acted silent movie. She has that "woe-is-me" expression.

A kid is also in the foreground. She's carrying a bouquet of flowers but seems to be completely distracted by the cool set of bones on the horse.

Christianity talks about eternal life and never dying, but what if God asks us to give that up? Is anybody willing to say "okay" to that kind of request? Is there anyone who is willing to let go over absolutely everything? The good and the bad?

I will gladly give up cotton in aspirin bottles and childproof bottles, but I'm going to have to think about giving up love and beauty and ribeye steaks cooked on pecan wood.

The Hanged Man card let our adventurer pause and absorb the universe. He had to face himself.

"How much do you want enlightenment?" the universe asked. The Fool responded by letting himself be hung upside down like a baby about to come out from the womb.

The instant follow-up is the Death card. It's like a quick inventory of some of the things the Fool will have to give up: everything. The whole kit and caboodle. He is asked to give up everything he can think of, everything the Lords of Karma can conjure, and junk from the his neighbors and cousins.

The Death card isn't about death. It's about how we deal with endings and beginnings. It is how we deal with change. It is about willingness.

I heard ordination described as being like the ordinand standing up before the Lords of Karma, snapping his/her fingers, and saying "Check please!"

There's nothing peaceful about jumping onto a path of spiritual growth. Those who walk that path — whether as a minister or mystic — just think they're getting into a life of peace and harmony. It's just the opposite.

Those in charge of the Karma Savings and Loan bundle up everything they can find. The Fool's is dumped on by all the cosmic crap in his own account, but it doesn't stop there. The Lords of Karma drag in people off the street and relieve them of all their karma baggage. The Fool get all their phlegm.

Helena Blavatsky write about her reaction to walking on the spiritual path. Her first reaction was how scary and awful the walk turned out to be. She wanted to run, to escape from the journey she chose. That was impossible. Once you start on the path, the universe keeps you there. Every time you try to escape, you get slapped back. There is no "easier, softer way" to use Alcoholics Anonymous terminology.

Madam Blavatsky says it felt like she would die from being crushed on the spiritual path. That's impossible, of course. Life itself is fatal. The spiritual journey isn't.

There was only one thing left for Blavatsky to do. She gave up, and that's when it happened. She let go absolutely, just like the Buddha did under the bodhi tree. He sat, seeking enlightenment, and it never came. Then he gave up, and poof: enlightenment in the flash of an eye.

Figure 12: H. P. Blavatsky (1831-1891)

> A flower blossoms; then withers and dies. It leaves fragrance behind, long after its delicate petals are but a little dust, still lingers in the air. Our material sense may not be cognizant of it, but it nevertheless exists.
>
> [Helena P. Blavatsky]

A. E. WAITE'S NOTES ON THE DEATH CARD

The veil or mask of life is perpetuated in change, transformation and passage from lower to higher, and this is more fitly represented in the rectified Tarot by one of the apocalyptic visions than by the crude notion of the reaping skeleton. Behind it lies the whole world of ascent in the spirit. The mysterious horseman moves slowly, bearing a black banner emblazoned with the Mystic Rose, which signifies life. Between two pillars on the verge of the horizon there shines the sun of immortality. The horseman carries no visible weapon, but king and child and maiden fall before him, while a prelate with clasped hands awaits his end.

There should be no need to point out that the suggestion of death, which I have made in connection with the previous card is, of course, to be understood mystically, but this is not the case in the present instance. The natural transit of man to the next stage of his being either is or may be one form of his progress, but the exotic and almost unknown entrance, while still in this life, into the state of mystical death is a change in the form of consciousness and the passage into a state to which ordinary death is neither the path nor gate. The existing occult explanations of the 13th card are, on the whole, better than usual, rebirth, creation, destination, renewal, and the rest.

Card 15. Temperance

> *The Bible tells us how to go to Heaven, not how the heavens go.*
> [Galileo Galilei (1564-1642)]

Aleister Crowley's version of the tarot doesn't have a Temperance card. Yes, he wasn't a very temperate fellow, but point is that he replaced Temperance with a card he called Alchemy.

The androgynous angel on Pamela Smith's Temperance card looks like it is following some alchemical formula. One foot is on the ground, and the other is in the water.[35] The angel is pouring something from the earth chalice into the water chalice. We add air to the formula when we see the angel's wings.

> *Submission and use of reason; that is what makes true Christianity.*
> [Blaise Pascal (1623-1662)]

In our case, "temperance" refers to the middle path. It's a little of this and a little of that.

There's a dirt path leading to the distant sun.

It's like Smith and Waite are screaming at us. The Fool just got through a couple of cards challenging his commitment to spiritual growth. And how we get a softer image about opposites. Earth flows through air and into water. Light and dark join together.

But if this is an alchemical formula, why is the angel eyeballing the amounts? Is the angel such an expert that measuring isn't required?

Maybe the angel suggesting we use trial and error.

Is the angel completely off the rail here?

Trial and error on a spiritual path that can mean eternal life. One wrong turn can put us on the path to hell.

---

[35] Metaphysical *Twister*! Sign me up!

I think the Fool is encouraged to experiment with life. He's already agreed to be willing to do everything. We know he really wants to be on this path. If spiritualism is alchemical, there's a formula. It may be there's no measurement because not everybody's formula will be the same. You may need blue syrup, while the Fool has to use green powder. Maybe the Fool is supposed to stir his pot with a twig of a pecan tree that died during a dust storm, and if you try such a twig you'll be changed into a left-handed giraffe being held captive in a Serbian zoo.

Alchemy is dangerous. Any spiritual path is dangerous. Our angelic admonition is to take each step with care. We're already on the spiritual path, but we can't just saunter along aimlessly. We can't copy somebody else's rules without testing them. One person may be convinced that you shouldn't eat shellfish. Another says you have to be circumcised. One group says being gay is the devil's work. Some may tell you that you can't be a soldier if you want to see heaven.

The angel on the Temperance Card is telling us to use the Scientific Method. The main component of this method is that the results get to be the best witness. It removes opinion and prejudice as much as they can be removed. Reliance on empirical methods go back to ancient Egypt, where they documented the movement of the stars and planets. Plato (Greece) tried to turn philosophy into science through logic (deductive reasoning).

Light is such an important metaphor for spiritual growth. Look at it with the eyes of science, and it gets uncanny. Consider light versus dark. Light moves along a path. Dark is just a blob. Light connects us to distant stars, and it blasts its way through the dark sky without effort.

> *Where is the way where light dwelleth? and as for darkness, where is the place thereof.*   [Job 38:19]

To be an inquiring mind in spiritual growth, here are the five fundamental steps of the Scientific Method:

1. Ask a question (Magician)

2. Research (Priestess)
3. Find a hypothesis (Lovers)
4. Test the hypothesis (Wheel of Fortune)
5. Analyze the data (Justice)

The mind-warping thing about the Scientific Method is that it isn't always iterative. If Step 4 throws errors, you go back to 2 or 3. Sometimes you don't really see the Grand Scheme because you're busy stumbling over the pieces.

Said in computer programmer terms: this is recursive descent.[36]

> There is a God-shaped vacuum in every heart.　　　[Blaise Pascal]

A. E. WAITE'S NOTES ON THE TEMPERANCE CARD

A winged angel, with the sign of the sun upon his forehead and on his breast the square and triangle of the septenary. I speak of him in the masculine sense, but the figure is neither male nor female. It is held to be pouring the essences of life from chalice to chalice. It has one foot upon the earth and one upon waters, thus illustrating the nature of the essences. A direct path goes up to certain heights on the verge of the horizon, and above there is a great light, through which a crown is seen vaguely. Hereof is some part of the Secret of Eternal Life, as it is possible to man in his incarnation. All the conventional emblems are renounced herein.

So also are the conventional meanings, which refer to changes in the seasons, perpetual movement of life and even the combination of ideas. It is, moreover, untrue to say that the figure symbolizes the genius of the sun, though it is the analogy of solar light, realized in the third part of our human triplicity. It is called Temperance fantastically, because, when the rule of it obtains in our consciousness, it tempers, combines and harmonizes the psychic and material natures. Under that rule we know in our rational part something of whence we came and whither we are going.

---

[36] This is a really funny observation, by the way. You pile on a bunch of tests, but things aren't clear until all the tests are run. They all unwind magically at the end, and you don't get any progress reports. The unwinding doesn't even look logical. It is the computer equivalent of *faith*. If you want to seem geeky to your friends, it's okay to laugh at "recursive descent."

Card 15. The Devil

> Resistance is futile. [Locutus, stardate: 45854.2]

"Live long and prosper," the Devil says as he does the Vulcan salute from Star Trek.

"Say what?" the people say. "Satan is from the planet Vulcan? Holy Mackerel, I had no idea."

The Devil in Pamela Smith's drawing isn't Satan. It's half goat and half creepy dude, which is how to describe Pan. He has an inverted (point downward) pentagram, which is used as the symbol of Satanism, the second degree of some Neopagan religions, and the Order of the Eastern Star (an offshoot of the Freemasons that admits both women and men).

The pentagram is a five-pointed star. I think of it representing people: head, two hands, and two feet. The inverted pentagram has the head as the lowest point, like the cross of St. Peter.

> Wherefore if thy hand or thy foot offend thee, cut them off, and cast them from thee: it is better for thee to enter into life halt or maimed, rather than having two hands or two feet to be cast into everlasting fire. And if thine eye offend thee, pluck it out, and cast it from thee: it is better for thee to enter into life with one eye, rather than having two eyes to be cast into hell fire. Take heed that ye despise not one of these little ones; for I say unto you, That in heaven their angels do always behold the face of my Father which is in heaven. For the Son of man is come to save that which was lost. [Matthew 18:8-11]

The card makes me yearn for the relative quiet of Temperance. Ah, those were the good old days, my friend. When we left Temperance's imagery, we left balance and the middle ground.

The card shows a woman sports a fashionable tail of grapes and grape leaves, while her boy toy has a tale that's burning. Ouch!

The man has his hand on his naked hip. I can just hear him saying "humph" to his captor.

Pan throws away concepts like finesse away like yesterday's garbage. I used to work for a guy like that. It was awful, and I felt shackled to that job for years. Go read "Deer in the Works," a short story by Kurt Vonnegut (1922-2007), for a splendid story about overcoming a dysfunctional job. It was published in his *Welcome to the Monkey House* anthology.[37]

Workers are chained to awful jobs. Spouses are forced to stay in abusive relationships because of something external (dogma, children, society, shame of failure).

> *For God so loved the world, that he gave his only begotten Son, that whosoever believeth in him should not perish, but have everlasting life.*　　　　　　　　　　　　　　　　　　　　　　[John 3:16]

---

[37] The story first appeared in Esquire magazine in April, 1955.

A. E. Waite's Notes on the Devil

The design is an accommodation, mean or harmony, between several motives mentioned in the first part. The Horned Goat of Mendes,[38] with wings like those of a bat, is standing on an altar. At the pit of the stomach there is the sign of Mercury. The right hand is upraised and extended, being the reverse of that benediction which is given by the Hierophant in the fifth card. In the left hand there is a great flaming torch, inverted towards the earth. A reversed pentagram is on the forehead. There is a ring in front of the altar, from which two chains are carried to the necks of two figures, male and female. These are analogous with those of the fifth card, as if Adam and Eve after the Fall. Hereof is the chain and fatality of the material life.

The figures are tailed, to signify the animal nature, but there is human intelligence in the faces, and he who is exalted above them is not to be their master for ever. Even now, he is also a bondsman, sustained by the evil that is in him and blind to the liberty of service. With more than his usual derision for the arts which he pre-

Figure 13: Benebdjedett

tended to respect and interpret as a master therein, Éliphas Lévi affirms that the Baphometic[39] figure is occult science and magic.   Another commentator says that in the Divine world it signifies predestination, but there is no correspondence in that world with the things, which below are of the brute. What it does signify is the Dweller on the Threshold without the Mystical Garden when those are driven forth therefrom who have eaten the forbidden fruit.

---

[38] Mendes is what the ancient Greeks called Egypt's town of Djedet. It was a center of religious practice, located in the Nile delta. One of the primary gods of Mendes was Banebdjedet, depicted as having a ram's head.

[39] The term Baphomet refers to the Banebdjedet-like figure on the Devil card. It became popular in the 1800s, but the word actually dates to a letter from Anselm of Ribemont, written in July, 1098.

Card 16. The Tower

And so it goes. The Fool finds himself yearning for the relative "peace" of the Devil when he first sees the Tower. At least everyone was alive on the previous card: chained but healthy.

The tower takes the idea of chains and exchanges it with people being thrown out of the tower. There are screams of terror. Film at eleven. The angst hasn't gone viral: this is full-bored bacterial.

Something blew the golden crown off its anchor. The crown (arrogance?) is thrown to earth along with the people.

The Fool didn't start here. It's been building. We saw sacrifice (Hanged Man). There was a stop for reflection on willingness (Death). The Fool saw moderation and science at Temperance. And it was damn the torpedoes with the "all in" nature of the Devil.

Things built up, and now they're exploding. This is all out war.

The edifice is crumbling or exploding.

> *Therefore whoever hears these sayings of Mine, and does them, I will liken him to a wise man who built his house on the rock: and the rain descended, the floods came, and the winds blew and beat on that house; and it did not fall, for it was founded on the rock. But everyone who hears these sayings of Mine, and does not do them, will be like a foolish man who built his house on the sand: and the rain descended, the floods came, and the winds blew and beat on that house; and it fell. And great was its fall.*
>
> [Matthew 7:24-27]

This is the rude awakening my grandmother used to warn about. Comeuppance. It's all circled back, and it is time to suffer for all the things I've done. I've been a cockroach, you know, and I've been crawling through the lives of others.

> *Just try and stay out of my way. Just try! I'll get you, my pretty, and your little dog, too!*
>
> [Wicked Witch of the West, *Wizard of Oz*]

When I first saw the Tower card, I got a serious fear of heights. I knew there was some evil creature (Thor and his lightening?) who was going to send lightening bolts to dislodge me from my secure life and send me falling onto the rocks below.

"It's nothing personal, kid," Thor would say. "It's just business. You wouldn't understand."

> *Fear not, little flock; for it is your Father's good pleasure to give you the kingdom.* [Luke 12:32]

The Tower card is a fairly recent addition to the major trump cards in the deck. The oldest decks don't have it. There are some card dating to the Middle Ages have a towerless tower, where people are running out of a burning one-story building.

Whether it's a ground-level building or a big stone tower, you have people being disrupted from their regular life. It is chaos. It is a frantic and explosive or corrosive change.

The kiddies and many adults get completely scared by The Tower. It's always my favorite card when my goodie-two-shoe cousins are around.

I was taught that crumbling towers were what to expect if I got uppity enough to challenge God's rule. They said it was the retribution of the God of the Old Testament.

> *I the Lord thy God am a jealous God, visiting the iniquity of the fathers upon the children unto the third and fourth generation of them that hate me.* [Exodus 20:5]

> *God is jealous, and the Lord revengeth; the Lord revengeth, and is furious; the Lord will take vengeance on his adversaries, and he reserveth wrath for his enemies.* [Naham 1:2]

My mother — God rest her soul — was a Southern Baptist. That's the protestant denomination formed after the rest of the

American Baptists passed policies against slavery. The Southern Baptists thought owning another person was just ducky. They've tempered that position since, but they continue to spew hatred. Jeremiah and the author of Leviticus has nothing on these people.

It just took me a couple of Sunday services with mommy to know that I needed to be elsewhere. Fortunately, my dad and his religious wanderings was a handy alternative.

The tower, I now believe, was an attempt to keep me in line. It was scary to a kid who had problems with authority. It was the fire and brimstone card to keep me from challenging the hegemony of established religion.

We pause now for the Fool to change his spandex leotards. He got so scared that he pooped all over himself.

And it was all for nothing. Nobody is going to get thrown out of any spiritual tower.

The Southern Baptists of my mother's generation are full of self-hate that has nothing to do with me. Jungian Psychology talks about the hatred of others being caused by our own Shadow Self. We have repressed weaknesses and shortcomings that we hate. We take out our own moral deficiencies on others, and that is somehow supposed to build us up.

There's the dreaded *Dark Night of the Soul*,[40] a scary place that mystics visit. That's probably what our traveler is experiencing. It is the dry terror with the very real feeling that God has abandoned us. We are so along. Our spirit is thrown out of the heavenly tower, and we are hurtling to the rocks below.

Contemplatives who have gone through this Dark Night report that it vanishes as fast as it appeared. That tells me it is an edifice of our own design. It is one of those play-pretties we keep in our mental toy box.

---

[40] A poem and a longer treatise by St. John of the Cross (1542-1591) that tells of the soul's journey into a deep mystical union with God.

The Dark Night — which seems so real — is an impostor that goes bump in the night. In the daylight, there's nothing to see. The Dark Night of mystics is a big vat of acid that strips everything from our soul.

An old woman — who had lots more wisdom than I'll ever see — turned the entire card around for me. She said I was relating to the people.

"You're the tower, son," she said. "God is cleansing you of impurities. You don't need a crown. You don't need kings with rules of behavior. You don't need diddley-squat."

> *I have found the paradox, that if you love until it hurts, there can be no more hurt, only more love.*
> [Mother Teresa of Calcutta (1910-1997)]

If I'm the tower, God has knocked it down, and that still hurts. Everything worldly has crumbled. I'm destroyed like the wicked witch in the Wizard of Oz. All that's left is some debris, strewn about on the rocks that had been my foundation.

This is cleansed. This is cleansed? We didn't just throw out the baby with the bathwater. We've discarded the bassinet and the family home.

When you get rid of everything, what's left is your willingness, and that's what God is looking for. The Tower is the scary cleansing that happens when we say OKAY to God and to the Lords of Karma.

The bad news is that if you're reading this book, you've probably already said OKAY. Sorry 'bout that.

The good news is that it'll work out. Eventually. Our story will have a happy ending. You didn't need all those creepy people and golden crowns muddling up your path. We are banishing everything: good, bad, ugly, pretty, baby, bathwater, baby poop, kitchen sink.

> *If you can keep your head when all about you*
> *Are losing theirs and blaming it on you;*
> *If you can trust yourself when all men doubt you,*

But make allowance for their doubting too:
If you can wait and not be tired by waiting,
Or being lied about, don't deal in lies,
Or being hated don't give way to hating,
And yet don't look too good, nor talk too wise;

If you can dream — and not make dreams your master;
If you can think — and not make thoughts your aim,
If you can meet with Triumph and Disaster
And treat those two impostors just the same:
If you can bear to hear the truth you've spoken
Twisted by knaves to make a trap for fools,
Or watch the things you gave your life to, broken,
And stoop and build 'em up with worn-out tools;

If you can make one heap of all your winnings
And risk it on one turn of pitch-and-toss,
And lose, and start again at your beginnings
And never breathe a word about your loss:
If you can force your heart and nerve and sinew
To serve your turn long after they are gone,
And so hold on when there is nothing in you
Except the Will which says to them: 'Hold on!'

If you can talk with crowds and keep your virtue,
Or walk with Kings — nor lose the common touch,
If neither foes nor loving friends can hurt you,
If all men count with you, but none too much:
If you can fill the unforgiving minute
With sixty seconds' worth of distance run,
Yours is the Earth and everything that's in it,
And — which is more — you'll be a Man, my son!

["If," Rudyard Kipling (1865-1936)]

A. E. WAITE'S NOTES ON THE TOWER CARD

Occult explanations attached to this card are meagre and mostly discon-
certing. It is idle to indicate that it depicts min in all its aspects, because it
bears this evidence on the surface. It is said further that it contains the first
allusion to a material building, but I do not conceive that the Tower is more
or less material than the pillars which we have met with in three previous
cases. I see nothing to warrant Papus[41] in supposing that it is literally the
fall of Adam, but there is more in favour of his alternative — that it signi-
fies the materialization of the spiritual word. The bibliographer Christian
imagines that it is the downfall of the mind, seeking to penetrate the mys-
tery of God. I agree rather with Grand Orient that it is the ruin of the
House of We, when evil has prevailed therein, and above all that it is the
rending of a House of Doctrine. I understand that the reference is, however,
to a House of Falsehood. It illustrates also in the most comprehensive way
the old truth that "except the Lord build the house, they labour in vain that
build it."

There is a sense in which the catastrophe is a reflection from the previous
card, but not on the side of the symbolism, which I have tried to indicate
therein. It is more correctly a question of analogy; one is concerned with the
fall into the material and animal state, while the other signifies destruction
on the intellectual side. The Tower has been spoken of as the chastisement
of pride and the intellect overwhelmed in the attempt to penetrate the
Mystery of God; but in neither case do these explanations account for the
two persons who are the living sufferers. The one is the literal word made
void and the other its false interpretation. In yet a deeper sense, it may sig-
nify also the end of a dispensation, but there is no possibility here for the
consideration of this involved question.

---

[41] Gérard Encausse (1865-1916) was a French occultist and hypnotist who used Papus as a penname. There is no known connection, but Papus was born on the same day that P. T. Barnum's big museum in Manhattan burned down. Coincidence? Synchronicity?

Card 17. The Star

Is anybody but me put off by that bird in the tree? It's a scrawny tree, and it's topped by the strangest bird that I ever saw.

If I were the Fool, I'd consider this comic relief. It's an antidote to the previous run of dismal sentiments. We have a woman who's nekkid-as-a-jaybird, and she isn't particularly beautiful. She has two tits but only one nipple. I'm not saying that it makes her a bad or substandard person, but the tarot cards have been idealistic. The woman is showing a little belly, and it isn't from pregnancy. She isn't slender or delicate. She's just a woman from the neighborhood, albeit dressed down from what most neighborhood ladies would do in polite society.

That bird is just too weird.

The woman is pouring liquid from two pitchers. One is sending nourishing water onto the ground (garden?). The other is putting water back into the pond (redundant, unnecessary).

She is apparently rewarded by little sprouts of plants on the ground. The have tiny red flowers, but they don't appear to be a rose bush or anything else you might grow for the bloom. They're weeds!

So for everybody keeping count... we have ourselves a fairly homely woman, naked and vulnerable and imperfect. She pours water both for good use (ground) and for silliness (pond). There's a gaunt bird that found its way to the top of a scrawny tree without the use of feathered flight.

> *Once upon a time there was a crooked tree and a straight tree. And they grew next to each other. And every day the straight tree would look at the crooked tree and he would say, "You're crooked. You've always been crooked and you'll continue to be crooked. But look at me! Look at me!" said the straight tree. He said, "I'm tall and I'm straight." And then one day the lumberjacks came into the forest and looked around, and the manager in charge said, "Cut all the straight trees." And that crooked tree is still there to this day, growing strong and growing strange.* [anonymous]

If he's smart, the Fool will see that what matters most is that he keeps trying. It isn't going to make things perfect.

I remember a story about Mother Teresa. Somebody was complaining to her about her work with the poor.

"How can you hope to be successful in helping the poor and the sick," he said. "You are poor and sick yourself."

"God didn't call me to be successful," she said. "He called me to be faithful."

But Mother Teresa did help thousands of people around Calcutta, and she inspired millions around the world. She did it while concentrating on the journey, not the destination.

If he's really smart, the Fool will pick up one further lesson from the Star: birds are intricate pieces of machinery. Not even God can build a good one when he's had too much wine or rum. Just sayin' — .

A. E. Waite's Notes on the Star Card

A great, radiant star of eight rays, surrounded by seven lesser stars — also of eight rays. The female figure in the foreground is entirely naked. Her left knee is on the land and her right foot upon the water. She pours Water of Life from two great ewers, irrigating sea and land. Behind her is rising ground and on the right a shrub or tree, whereon a bird alights. The figure expresses eternal youth and beauty. The star is l'étoile flamboyante,[42] which appears in Masonic symbolism, but has been confused therein. That which the figure communicates to the living scene is the substance of the heavens and the elements. It has been said truly that the mottoes of this card are "Waters of Life freely" and "Gifts of the Spirit."

The summary of several tawdry explanations says that it is a card of hope. On other planes it has been certified as immortality and interior light. For the majority of prepared minds, the figure will appear as the type of Truth unveiled, glorious in undying beauty, pouring on the waters of the soul some part and measure of her priceless possession. But she is in reality the Great Mother in the Kabalistic Sephira Binah, which is supernal Understanding, who communicates to the Sephiroth that are below in the measure that they can receive her influx.

---

[42] the blazing star

Card 18. The Moon

Two columns on the horizon again. Again! Where's Pixie Smith? I need a word with her.

Our vantage point is a pond. That is the point of view of the Fool on this card. If we are seeing the journey of the vagabond, he's looking at the moon from a pool of reflective water. This is the nebulous culmination of his Dark Night.

> *Either you repeat the same conventional doctrines everybody is saying, or else you say something true, and it will sound like it's from Neptune.* [Noam Chomsky (b1928)]

We have a drawing of the Moon in the distance. The "man" in the moon looks like a pensive woman who is crying all over the sky. Each teardrop is a "yod" (yodh) — a character in the Hebrew alphabet. It's part of the IHVH, the Tetragrammaton (literally 'four letters'), one of the names of God.[43]

Figure 14: Yod

Two yods together are the abbreviation of the word Adonai ("lord").

The creatures on the Moon card are going nuts, like they're having a bad LSD experience or something. An orange dog is wailing at the moon. A yellow dog has his lips convoluted in a kind of growl.

And what in the world would possess a lobster to come crawling out of the water. Wait, the lobster is red, and that means it's already cooked. It could be just floating on the water, not crawling.

All we need is some mist or fog to complete the image of the netherworld.

Several other cards — Chariot, Hierophant, and Temperance — have shown us logic. This isn't one of those cards. The Moon is that dreamy trance we get sometimes. It is about intuition, not scientific

---

[43] YOD is also the airport designation of Cold Lake, a base used by the Royal Canadian Air Force. I'm going out on a limb and say that's not what Pamela Smith was reaching for.

discovery. It can lead to crazy behavior and embarrassing situations in addition to the wonderful serendipity of intuition.

> The only real valuable thing is intuition.
>
> [Albert Einstein (1879-1955)]

> Often you have to rely on intuition.
>
> [Bill Gates (b1955)]

This is the card of music and art. It is the card about personal preferences and taste. If you are doing something that attracts an orange dog and a lobster, I am going to give you plenty of space to explore the beat of that different drummer. I have no right to say your taste in dogs and lobsters is somehow inferior. Yeah, it probably is, but I have no right to say so.

"It's wrong to like strawberries," the grumpy old guy says.

"*De gustibus non est disputandum*," I retort quickly with a nasal snort and a rude flick of my wrist.

"The hell?" the man asks as he takes a step back to protect himself.

"Latin saying that means taste is not disputable."

"Why in tarnation didn't you just say so?" he growls.

"If I say that I like strawberries, the subject is closed."

"Ain't," he hisses, spitting through his ill-fitting dentures.

"Is, and there's no one set of tastes that's more correct than other sets."

The exception here is ribeye. It's the obvious exception. I deny the legitimacy of anybody's right to dislike a ribeye steak. Period. I once fired a doctor for telling me to cut back on red meat.[44]

---

[44] Oh, yes I did too.

A good traveler has no fixed plan, and is not intent on arriving.
[Lao-tzu (640 BCE - ?)]

So what is the Fool supposed to do with intuition? Can he know things that can't be known? Can he have preferences and tastes that make him look bonkers to everyone else?

A. E. WAITE'S NOTES ON THE MOON CARD

The distinction between this card and some of the conventional types is that the moon is increasing on what is called the side of mercy, to the right of the observer. It has sixteen chief and sixteen secondary rays. The card represents life of the imagination apart from life of the spirit. The path between the towers is the issue into the unknown. The dog and wolf are the fears of the natural mind in the presence of that place of exit, when there is only reflected light to guide it.

The last reference is a key to another form of symbolism. The intellectual light is a reflection and beyond it is the unknown mystery which it cannot shew forth. It illuminates our animal nature, types of which are represented below — the dog, the wolf and that which comes up out of the deeps, the nameless and hideous tendency which is lower than the savage beast. It strives to attain manifestation, symbolized by crawling from the abyss of water to the land, but as a rule it sinks back whence it came. The face of the mind directs a calm gaze upon the unrest below; the dew of thought falls; the message is: Peace, be still; and it may be that there shall come a calm upon the animal nature, while the abyss beneath shall cease from giving up a form.

Card 19. The Sun

> *More radiant than the sun, purer than the snow, subtler than the ether, is the self, the spirit within my heart. I am that self; that self am I.* [Charles W. Leadbeater (1914-1934)]

How does a white horse stay so white under the rays of the sun? My Scandinavian skin would turn beet-red in no time.

There's a naked adolescent riding the horse without a saddle, and the kid doesn't seem to know he/she is supposed to be holding on for dear life. "Here I am," the kid seems to say.

In the background is a tall wall of cinderblocks. It's been turned into a planter for sunflowers. The sunflowers are in protest because they're facing away from the sun. The artist knows nothing about sunflowers, I suppose.

"De gustibus — ," Pixie Smith tells me from her grave.

"What kind of child are you?" the Fool asks.

"I'm you," the kid says. "Come on outside. It's warm and fun."

"Don't mess with me," the fool says. "You're a kid. I'm an adult."

"Don't you feel like a kid inside?"

"Sometimes," the Fool admits sheepishly.

> *The disciples unto Jesus, saying, Who is the greatest in the kingdom of heaven? And Jesus called a little child unto him, and set him in the midst of them, And said, Verily I say unto you, Except ye be converted, and become as little children, ye shall not enter into the kingdom of heaven. Whosoever therefore shall humble himself as this little child, the same is greatest in the kingdom of heaven. And whoso shall receive one such little child in my name receiveth me. But whoso shall offend one of these little ones which believe in me, it were better for him that a millstone were hanged about his neck, and that he were drowned in the depth of the sea.*
>
> [Matthew 18:1-6]

A mystic once got me to do a simple yet powerful exercise to get me in touch with my inner child. I made the room dark, except for one candle. I sat on the floor in the nude. I was in front of a mirror that I had leaned up against the wall. The mystic told me to stare at myself. That was hard because I have this fantasy about physical things that reality completely destroys, if you know what I mean. It made me uncomfortable for a long time, but I stuck it out. The mystic told me to stare into the reflection of my own eyes. I looked into my own eyes. After the longest time, I repeated what the mystic told me to say: "I love you. I need you. Be with me. Help me."

It sounds simple, but it's one of the most powerful things I ever did.

> *Walk while ye have the light, lest darkness come upon you: for he that walketh in darkness knoweth not whither he goeth. While ye have light, believe in the light, that ye may be the children of light.*
> [John 12:35-36]

If the moon is murky, the sun is clarity. The sun rises and the child invites us to the East, the traditional location of the altar in Christian churches. The priest in a traditional service appears to have his back to the people, but that's a misunderstanding. All eyes are on the sunrise during the Mass. The priest and the people all face the same direction.

Although we have sunflowers, I don't think this is an outside sun in the summer. I think the light is the inner light.

> *May the Holy Ones, whose pupils you aspire to become, show you the Light you seek, give you the strong aid of their compassion and their wisdom. There is a peace that passeth understanding; it abides in the hearts of those who live in the Eternal; there is a power that maketh all things new; it lives and moves in those who know the Self as One. May that peace brood over you, that power uplift you, till you stand where the One Initiator is invoked, till you*

see *His Star shine forth.*
["First Ray Benediction" by Annie Besant, Liberal Catholic liturgy]

A. E. WAITE'S NOTES ON THE SUN CARD

The naked child mounted on a white horse and displaying a red standard has been mentioned already as the better symbolism connected with this card. It is the destiny of the Supernatural East and the great and holy light which goes before the endless procession of humanity, coming out from the walled garden of the sensitive life and passing on the journey home. The card signifies, therefore, the transit from the manifest light of this world, represented by the glorious sun of earth, to the light of the world to come, which goes before aspiration and is typified by the heart of a child.

But the last allusion is again the key to a different form or aspect of the symbolism. The sun is that of consciousness in the spirit - the direct as the antithesis of the reflected light. The characteristic type of humanity has become a little child therein — a child in the sense of simplicity and innocence in the sense of wisdom. In that simplicity, he bears the seal of Nature and of Art; in that innocence, he signifies the restored world. When the self-knowing spirit has dawned in the consciousness above the natural mind, that mind in its renewal leads forth the animal nature in a state of perfect conformity.

Card 20. Judgement

> Heaven and earth shall pass away. [Matthew 24:35]

It was a challenge to keep Judgement spelled with an "e." My editor kept trying to change it to Judgment. The spell-checker in my word processor went completely nuts every time I typed it.

Judgement is how Arthur Waite and Pixie Smith spelled the word back in the early 20th century.

> England and America are two countries separated by a common language. [George Bernard Shaw (1856-1950)]

What is it with these cards? I was feeling good about my spiritual journey toward the inner light of the sun (Son).

Here comes some kind of bugle playing by Gabriel. Sometimes Gabriel seems to be male, but then it morphs into a female. This is one confusing angel.

If the angel is borderline confusing, the music must have been downright disturbing. I'm guessing operetta or angelic disco as sung by a coloratura.

Whatever the tune might be, it is forcing all the dead people to stand up and wave their arms.

"Stop it!" they scream through necks contorted by the melody.

The Fool has been through so much. Just as he thinks that he's arriving at the end of the journey, he's jarred by the noise.

There are dead people everywhere.

Something that isn't said is that I think the Fool is actually facing himself. The men, women, and children who are shaken from their slumber are really the Fool. It could be previous lives (reincarnation was taught in the early Christian church). It could be old attitudes and personas of the Fool's current life.

The zombies may be all those people ejected back at The Tower card. If that's the case, you may have some explaining to do.

"Hey, Fool," the zombies say, "how come you threw us out of your tower?"

And then they start moving toward you menacingly. With tarot cards, it's never what you think. The meaning keeps changing. What seemed so awful (Tower) is really cleansing. Judgement is where the Lords of Karma keep the universe in balance. If you see anything sweet, run like your life depends on it.

> Well-ordered self-love is right and natural.
> [Thomas Aquinas (1225-1274)]

Regardless of the explanation of these rising zombies, the Fool is looking at himself. Remembering himself. Seeing that his shadow states aren't that gruesome.

> There are three side effects of [LSD]: enhanced long-term memory, decreased short-term memory, and I forget the third.
> [Timothy Leary]

In some other tarot decks, the angel is replaced by Hermes (Mercury), the god associated with messages.

This is tarot. If you see Tarot-Hermes on "Caller ID," let it roll over to voicemail. You'll thank me later.

A. E. Waite's Notes on the Judgement Card

I have said that this symbol is essentially invariable in all Tarot sets, or at least the variations do not alter its character. The great angel is here encompassed by clouds, but he blows his bannered trumpet, and the cross as usual is displayed on the banner. The dead are rising from their tombs — a woman on the right, a man on the left hand, and between them their child, whose back is turned. But in this card there are more than three who are restored, and it has been thought worth while to make this variation as illustrating the insufficiency of current explanations. It should be noted that all the figures are as one in the wonder, adoration and ecstasy expressed by their attitudes. It is the card which registers the accomplishment of the great work of transformation in answer to the summons of the Supernal — which summons is heard and answered from within.

Herein is the intimation of a significance, which cannot well be carried further in the present place. What is that within us, which does sound a trumpet and all that is lower in our nature rises in response — almost in a moment, almost in the twinkling of an eye? Let the card continue to depict, for those who can see no further, the Last judgment and the resurrection in the natural body; but let those who have inward eyes look and discover therewith. They will understand that it has been called truly in the past a card of eternal life, and for this reason it may be compared with that which passes under the name of Temperance.

Card 21. The World

Pamela Smith has put our traveler inside a yoni of laurel leaves for the last stop, and he's sprouted breasts for this final class picture. That tells us something about Pamela Smith, or the Fool, or about gender itself. I'm not sure which, to tell you the truth.

It is definitely a card full of female energies. The yoni is the Sanskrit word for vagina, and it's used the same way the phallus is used for male energies. In the case of the World card, I think the yoni is the gateway to a new world. The character is dancing inside it, skipping along.

The four creatures of the zodiac are back for another engagement. We first saw them at the Wheel of Fortune. The previous card used the animals to show that things can pop up at random or as a sequence. They are here with the World card to show that everything belongs to the Fool.

She has twirling batons like she is from the marching band of an American university. She may not be wearing the band's approved uniform, but that's just a detail.

In a very real sense, the World card and the Fool card are the same. The Fool is nonchalantly walking off a cliff with no particular reason. The World card has a woman skipping around inside a mystical vagina, and if you can come up with a reason for that behavior, then you're stodgier than me.

> Yes, we are going around in circles. But you see, going around in circles — as you may have observed by looking at the sky — is what the universe is doing!   [Alan Watts (1915-1973)]

The central figure of The World card looks like she's dancing, and that's a wonderful way to complete the Fool's journey. She isn't walking along a path to get from Point A to Point B. She is dancing.

> The right art is purposeless, aimless! The more obstinately you try to learn how to shoot the arrow for the sake of hitting the goal, the less you will succeed in the one and the further the other will recede.   [D. T. Suzuki (1870-1966)]

It's quite pointless. It's also wonderful. It is meaningless meaning. It is enlightened play. We are all on a cosmic dance, and some of us can't help but bump into furniture and step on toes.

It's important that we make our journey. God seems to need or want every one of us. You do this, and I do that. I have no idea what He has in store for me or you or anybody else, but together we make the great mystical dance. God sees merit in the dance, even when I bump into things.

When you fall, I hope that I'll be there like a bodhisattva to help you up. It's nothing person, but I will probably be giggling at your clumsiness because I will see a reflection of my own antics.

> *'Will you walk a little faster?' said a whiting to a snail,*
>
> *"There's a porpoise close behind us, and he's treading on my tail.*
>
> *See how eagerly the lobsters and the turtles all advance!*
>
> *They are waiting on the shingle – will you come and join the dance?*
>
> *Will you, won't you, will you, won't you, will you join the dance?*
>
> [Lewis Carroll, "Mock Turtle song," *Alice in Wonderland*[45]]

Figure 16: Gryphon, Alice, Mock Turtle (John Tenniel, 1865)

If I take anything worthwhile from joining the Fool on his journey is that his journey to God that would absolutely kill me! I could not walk those same steps or make those stops along the way without ending up in prison, the hospital, and the morgue.

We all take this journey in one form or another. As spiritual beings, we're compelled. Some of us are obsessed by it (monks, priests,

---

[45] 1865

sisters). A few are lucky enough to learn to have fun with it (Saint Symeon Salas).

When we stumble, we get "do-overs." In English, we have an expression that says *practice makes perfect*. Balderdash. In Germany, there's a much better version:

> *Übung macht den Meister.*
> Repetition makes the master.

I'm happy with progress, and I will leave perfection to the saints.

> *Our hearts are ever restless until they find their rest in Him.*
>
> [Augustine of Hippo (354-430)]

This is the Fool's journey. Foolish, maybe. But it is all his journey. What I get from watching his adventure is that my own adventure has value. I'm probably going to get the various waypoints done in a different sequence because nobody's journey is exactly the same. It will be my sequence, and my adventure would probably send the Fool to the hospital or the morgue.

Neither you nor I have standing to complain about his journey. He can't complain about ours. Anything that says my path to God is wrong or less deserving has missed the whole point.

> *Christianity is one of the great paths up the mountain of light at the summit of which sits God Himself. It is one of the paths, but only one, and if we have a number of people all round the base of the mountain, the shortest path to the top for each man is the path, which opens before him. It would be foolish to have the idea that we must go and drag a man all round the base of the mountain in order to make him walk up our particular path.*
> [Charles W. Leadbeater, Hidden Side of Christian Festivals]

Amen.

A. E. Waite's Notes on the World Card

As this final message of the Major Trumps is unchanged — and indeed unchangeable — in respect of its design, it has been partly described already regarding its deeper sense. It represents also the perfection and end of the Cosmos, the secret which is within it, the rapture of the universe when it understands itself in God. It is further the state of the soul in the consciousness of Divine Vision, reflected from the self-knowing spirit. But these meanings are without prejudice to that which I have said concerning it on the material side.

It has more than one message on the macrocosmic side and is, for example, the state of the restored world when the law of manifestation shall have been carried to the highest degree of natural perfection. But it is perhaps more especially a story of the past, referring to that day when all was declared to be good, when the morning stars sang together and all the Sons of God shouted for joy. One of the worst explanations concerning it is that the figure symbolizes the Magus when he has reached the highest degree of initiation; another account says that it represents the absolute, which is ridiculous. The figure has been said to stand for Truth, which is, however, more properly allocated to the seventeenth card. Lastly, it has been called the Crown of the Magi.

Appendix

SEPHER YETZIRAH

Translated by W. Wynn Westcott (1887)

The Book of Creation of Kabala

I

1. In two and thirty most occult and wonderful paths of wisdom did JAH the Lord of Hosts engrave his name: God of the armies of Israel, ever-living God, merciful and gracious, sublime, dwelling on high, who inhabiteth eternity. He created this universe by the three Sepharim, Number, Writing, and Speech.

2. Ten are the numbers, as are the Sephiroth, and twenty-two the letters, these are the Foundation of all things. Of these letters, three are mothers, seven are double, and twelve are simple.

3. The ten numbers formed from nothing are the Decad: these are seen in the fingers of the hands, five on one, five on the other, and over them is the Covenant by voice spiritual, and the rite of Circumcision, corporeal (as of Abraham).

4. Ten are the numbers of the ineffable Sephiroth, ten and not nine, ten and not eleven. Learn this wisdom, and be wise in the understanding of it, investigate these numbers, and draw knowledge from them, fix the design in its purity, and pass from it to its Creator seated on his throne.

5. These Ten Numbers, beyond the Infinite one, have the boundless realms, boundless origin and end, an abyss of good and one of evil, boundless height and depth, East and West, North and South, and the one only God and king, faithful forever seated on his throne, shall rule over all, forever and ever.

6. These ten Sephiroth which are ineffable, whose appearance is like scintillating flames, have no end but are infinite. The word of God is in them as they burst forth, and as they return;

they obey the divine command, rushing along as a whirlwind, returning to prostrate themselves at his throne.

7. These ten Sephiroth which are, moreover, ineffable, have their end even as their beginning, conjoined, even as is a flame to a burning coal: for our God is superlative in his unity, and does not permit any second one. And who canst thou place before the only one?

8. And as to this Decad of the Sephiroth, restrain thy lips from comment, and thy mind from thought of them, and if thy heart fail thee return to thy place; therefore is it written, "The living creatures ran and returned," and on this wise was the covenant made with us.

9. These are the ten emanations of number. One is the Spirit of the Living God, blessed and more than blessed be the name of the Living God of Ages. The Holy Spirit is his Voice, his Spirit, and his Word.

10. Second, from the Spirit he made Air and formed for speech twenty-two letters, three of which are mothers, A, M, SH, seven are double, B, G, D, K, P, R, T, and twelve are single, E, V, Z, CH, H, I, L, N, S, O, Tz, Q, but the spirit is first among these. Third, Primitive Water. He also formed and designed from his Spirit, and from the void and formless made earth, even as a rampart, or standing wall, and varied its surface even as the crossing of beams. Fourth, from the Water, He designed Fire, and from it formed for himself a throne of honor, with Auphanim, Seraphim, Holy Animals, and ministering Angels, and with these he formed his dwelling, as is written in the text "Who maketh his angels spirits and his ministers a flaming fire." (Psalm civ. 4.)

11. He selected three letters from the simple ones, and sealed them as forming his great Name, IHV and he sealed the universe in six directions.

- Five.- He looked above, and sealed the height, with IHV.
- Six.- He looked below, and sealed the deep, with IVH.
- Seven.- He looked forward, and sealed the East, with HIV.
- Eight.-He looked backward, and sealed the West, with VHI.

- Nine.- He looked to the right, and sealed the South, with VIH.
- Ten.-He looked to the left, and sealed the North, with HV1.

12. These are the ten ineffable existences, the spirit of the living God, Air, Water, Fire, Height and Depth, East and West, North and South.

||

1. The foundations are the twenty-two letters, three mothers, seven double, and twelve single letters. Three mothers, namely A, M, SH, these are Air, Water, and Fire: Mute as Water, Hissing as Fire, and Air of a spiritual type, is as the tongue of a balance standing erect between them pointing out the equilibrium which exists.

2. He hath formed, weighed, transmuted, composed, and created with these twenty-two letters every living being, and every soul yet uncreated.

3. Twenty-two letters are formed by the voice, impressed on the air, and audibly uttered in five situations, in the throat, guttural sounds; in the palate, palatals; by the tongue, linguals; through the teeth, dentals; and by the lips, labial sounds.

4. These twenty-two letters, the foundations, He arranged as on a sphere, with two hundred and thirty-one modes of entrance. If the sphere be rotated forward, good is implied, if in a retrograde manner evil is intended.

5. For He indeed showed the mode of combination of the letters, each with each, Aleph with all, and all with Aleph. Thus in combining all together in pairs are produced these two hundred and thirty-one gates of knowledge. And from Nothingness did He make something, and all forms of speech and every created thing, and from the empty void He made the solid earth, and from the non-existent He brought forth Life.

6. He hewed, as it were, immense column or colossal pillars, out of the intangible air, and from the empty space. And this is the impress of the whole, twenty-one letters, all from one the Aleph.

III

1.   The three mother letters A, M, SH are the foundations of the whole; and resemble a Balance, the good in one scale, the evil in the other, and the oscillating tongue of the Balance between them.

2.   These three mothers enclose a mighty mystery, most occult and most marvelous, sealed as with six rings, and from them proceed primeval Fire, Water, and Air; these are subsequently differentiated into male and female. At first existed these three mothers, and there arose three masculine powers, and hence all things have originated.

3.   The three mothers are A, M, SH; and in the beginning as to the Macrocosm the Heavens were created from Fire; the Earth from primeval Water; and the Air was formed from the Spirit, which stands alone in the midst, and is the Mediator between them.

4.   In the Year or as regards Time, these three mothers represent Heat, Cold, and a Temperate climate, the heat from the fire, the cold from the water, and the temperate state from the spiritual air which again is an equalizer between them.

5.   These three mothers again represent in the Microcosm or Human form, male and female; the Head, the Belly, and the Chest; the bead from the fire, the belly from water, and the chest from the air lieth between them.

6.   These three mothers did he create, form, and design, and combine with the three mothers in the world, and in the year, and in Man, both male and female.

- He caused Aleph to reign in the air, and crown it, and combined one with the other, and with these he sealed the Air in the world, the temperate climate of the year, and the chest (the lungs for breathing air) in man; the male with A, M, SH, the female with SH, M, A. He caused Mem to predominate in Water, and crowned it, and combined it with others, and formed Earth on the world, cold in the year, and the fruit of the womb in mankind, being carried in the belly.

- He caused Shin to reign in Fire and crowned it, and he combined one with the other, and sealed them, as heaven in the universe, as heat in the year, and as the head of Man and Woman.

IV

1. There were formed seven double letters, Beth, Gimel, Daleth, Kaph, Pe, Resh, Tau, each has two voices, either aspirated or softened. These are the foundations of Life, Peace, Riches, Beauty or Reputation, Wisdom, Fruitfulness, and Power. These are double, because their opposites take part in life, opposed to Life is Death; to Peace, War; to Riches, Poverty; to Beauty or Reputation, Deformity or Disrepute; to Wisdom, Ignorance; to Fruitfulness, Sterility; to Power, Slavery.

2. These seven double letters point out the dimensions, East, West, height, depth, North, South, with the holy temple in the middle, sustaining all things.

3. These seven double letters He formed, designed, created, and combined into the Stars of the Universe, the days of the week, the orifices of perception in man; and from them he made seven heavens, and seven planets, all from nothingness, and, moreover, he has preferred and blessed the sacred Heptad.

4. From two letters, or forms He composed two dwellings; from three, six; from four, twenty-four; from five, one hundred and twenty; from six, seven hundred and twenty; from seven, five thousand and forty; and from thence their numbers increase in a manner beyond counting; and are incomprehensible. These seven are Planets of the Universe, the Sun, Venus, Mercury, Moon, Saturn, Jupiter, and Mars; the seven days are the days of creation; and these an the seven gateways of a man, two eyes, two ears, two nostrils and a mouth, through which he perceives by his senses.

V

1. The simple letters are twelve, namely: He, Vau, Zain, Heth, Teth, Yod, Lamed, Nun, Samech, Oin, Tzaddi, and Quoph; they represent the fundamental properties, eight, hearing, smell, speech, desire for food, the sexual appetite, movement,

anger, mirth, thought, sleep, and work. These symbolize also twelve directions in space: northeast, southeast, the east above, the east below, the northwest, southwest, the west above, the west below, the upper south, the lower south, the upper north, the lower north. These diverge to all eternity, and an as the arms of the universe.

2. These twelve letters, he designed, formed, combined, weighed, and changed, and created with them the twelve divisions of the heavens (namely, the zodiacal constellations), the twelve months of the year, and the twelve important organs of the frame of man, namely the right and left hands, the right and left feet, two kidneys, the liver, the gall, the spleen, the intestines, the gullet, and the stomach.

3. Three mothers, seven double and twelve simple, these are the twenty-two letters with which I H V H Tetragrammaton, that is our Lord of Hosts, exalted, and existed in the ages, whose name is Holy, created three fathers, fire and spirit and water, progressing beyond them, seven heavens with their armies of angels; and twelve limits of the universe.

VI

1. In proof of these things, and witnessing faithfully are the Universe, the Year of time, and Man himself, the Microcosm. He fixed these as testimonies of the Triad, the Heptad, and the Dodecad; the twelve constellations rulers of the world, the Dragon (THELE) Tali which environs the universe, and the microcosm, man.

   • The triad, fire, water, and air; the fire above, the water below, and the air in the midst. The proof of which is that air is a participator with both.

2. Tali, the Dragon, is above the Universe, as a king on his throne; the sphere in the year as a king in his State, the Heart of man as a king in warfare.

   • And our God made the states of opposition, good and evil, good from the good, and evil from the evil. Happiness is reserved for the just, and misery for the wicked ones.

3. And out of the triad one stands apart; and in the heptad there are two triads, and one standing apart. The dodecad symbolizes war, the triad of amity, the triad of enmity, three which are life-giving, three which are death-dealing, and God, the faithful king, rules over all from the throne of his sanctity.

   - One above three, three above seven, and seven above twelve, and all are linked together, and one with another.

4. After that our father Abraham had seen, and pondered over, investigated, and understood these things, he designed, engraved, and composed them, and received them into his power (hands). Then the Lord of all appeared unto him, made a covenant with him, and kissed his head, and naming him after his own name, called him his friend; and as it is written, completed a covenant with him and with his seed forever, who then believed on God, the Tetragrammaton, and it was imputed to him for righteousness.

   - God ordained a covenant between the toes of his feet, that of circumcision; and a covenant between the fingers of his hands, that of the Tongue. He bound the essences of the twenty-two letters on his tongue, and God disclosed to him the secrets of them. God has carried these through waters, He has borne them aloft through fire, and He has stamped them in the storms of the air; He has distributed them among the seven stars, and has assigned them to twelve celestial constellations. Amen.

CORRESPONDENCES

Card	Hebrew	Music	Direction
00 The Fool	Aleph א	E	Above -> Below
01 Magician	Bet ב	E	Above
02 Priestess	Gimel ג	G#	Below
03 Empress	Dalet ד	F#	East
04 Emperor	Heh ה	C	Northeast
05 Hierophant	Vau ו	C#	Southeast
06 Lovers	Zain ז	D	East-above
07 Chariot	Chet ח	D#	East-below
08 Strength	Tet ט	E	North-above
09 Hermit	Yod י	F	North-below
10 Wheel	Kaph כ	A#	West
11 Justice	Lamed ל	G#	Northwest
12 Hanged Man	Mem מ	G#	East-West
13 Death	Nun נ	G	Southwest
14 Temperance	Samekh ס	G#	West-above
15 Devil	Ayin ע	A	West-below
16 Tower	Peh פ	C	North
17 Star	Tzaddi צ	A#	South-above
18 Moon	Qof ק	B	South-below
19 Sun	Resh ר	D	South
20 Judgement	Shin ש	C	North-South
21 World	Taw ת	A	Central

The Hebrew letter associations are from numerous sources, including the Golden Dawn. The musical notes came through Rev. Paul F. Case (1884-1954), a Liberal Catholic priest and founder of the Builders of the Adytum. Directions were shown in Sepher Yetzirah, a Kabalistic book of Jewish mysticism that dates to about 200 BCE.

COLORS

Blue

- Peace
- Flow of understanding
- Calmness

Yellow

- Thought
- Memory
- Direct clarity
- The "left brain"
- Decisions

Red

- Passion
- Energy
- Enthusiasm

Orange

- Combines yellow + red
- Play
- Balance
- Creativity

Green

- Grounding
- Growth and life
- Health
- Abundance (crops, etc)
- Harmony

Indigo (new blue jeans)

- Wisdom
- Enlightenment
- Intuition
- Self-understanding

Violet

- Deep violet is associated with sorrow
- Purple hues are about spiritual enlightenment
- Bluish hues are about idealism
- Mental health
- Inspiration

Bibliography

Anonymous. *Alcoholics Anonymous: The Big Book*, 4th Edition. 978-1893007178. AA World Services, 2002.

Case, Paul Foster. *The Tarot: A Key to the Wisdom of the Ages*. 978-1585424917. Tarcher, 2006.

Hall, Manly P. *The Secret Teachings of All Ages*. 1-60459-095-5. Wilder Press, 2009.

Huets, Jean and Kaplan, Stuart R. *The Encyclopedia of Tarot*. 978-0913866115. US Games, 1978.

Irenaeus. *Scandal of the Incarnation: Irenaeus Against the Heresies*. 978-0898703153. St. Ignatius Press, 1990.

Krueger, Derek. *Symeon the Holy Fool*. 0520089111. University California Berkeley, 1996.

Leadbeater, Charles W. *Hidden Side of Christian Festivals*. 978-1477489093. Mystic Ways Books, 2012.

Merton, Thomas, *New Seeds of Contemplation*. 978-0811217248. New Directions, 2007.

Nichols, Sallie. *Jung and Tarot: An Archetypal Journey*. 978-0877285151. Weiser Books, 1980.

Smith, Pamela Colman. *Annancy Stories*. 978-0976961222. Darker Intentions Press, 2006.

Waite, Arthur E. *Holy Kabbalah, The*. 978-1602063242. Cosimo Classics, 2007

Waite, Arthur E. *Original Rider Waite Tarot Pack, The*. 978-0880796866. US Games, 1993.

Watts, Alan. *The Book: On the Taboo Against Knowing Who You Are*. 978-0679723004. Vintage Books, 1989.

Westcott, W. Wynn. *Sepher Yetzirah*. page 125 above

ABOUT THE AUTHOR

Figure 17: Abp. Wynn Wagner

Archbishop Wynn Wagner is the Coadjutor Emeritus of the North American Old Catholic Church. His regional responsibilities included all of the territory from Florida to Texas. He is also the retired president of the World Conference of Old Catholic Churches.

Yes, his former colleagues and co-workers in the Old Catholic Church cringe a little when they hear the archbishop has written another book. Yes, they most likely rolled their eyes when they heard this was about tarot. No, Abp. Wynn doesn't really care about what bishops might do with their respective eyes or eyebrows. They can spit and grunt 'til the cows come home, for Pete's sake. He wrote a <u>four</u>-part trilogy, so a bishop rolling his/her eyes is little more than a rounding error.

Before he was an archbishop, he earned a living as a computer programmer. In addition to helping write tax software used by the largest corporations in America, he also founded OPUS, a computer bulletin-board system (BBS) in the 1980s. OPUS was a forerunner of the Internet. It was the most popular BBS in history. One remarkable thing about OPUS is that Wynn never made a penny from its sale. He asked users to donate money to their local HIV/AIDS charity. OPUS raised millions of dollars for those charities around the world at a time when no government and few individuals were doing anything to help those suffering from the pandemic.

He was the 2012 recipient of the AEGiS Health, Human Rights and Human Services Award. The award marks a lifetime of humanitarian work. "The truly remarkable thing is that your informational advice has been coupled with spiritual encouragement and hope. Science and Spirit have worked so well [together]," Sister Mary Elizabeth, the founder of AEGiS, said in announcing the award.

LIST OF FIGURES

INDEX

OTHER TITLES FROM MYSTIC WAYS BOOKS

A Catechism of the Liberal Catholic Church (ISBN 978–1453840245). Fourth edition. Archbishop Wynn Wagner (2010)

A Pilgrim's Guide to the Old Catholic Church (ISBN 978–1449992798) (2009)

A Textbook of Theosophy (ISBN 978-1477500644) Abp. Charles W. Leadbeater (1912, 2012)

Canons of the North American Old Catholic Church (ISBN 978–1-4499–9610-9) (2009)

Eucharist (Sacramentary) (ISBN 978–0-5572–1970-4) (2010)

Hidden Side of Christian Festivals (ISBN 978-1477489093) Abp. Charles W. Leadbeater (1912, 2012)

Ordo Missae (pew) (ISBN 978–0-5572–1997-1) (2009)

Recovering Catholic or "How to be Catholic without being Roman Catholic" (ISBN 978–1-4505–1149-0) Archbishop Wynn Wagner (2009)

Sanctification of Time (ISBN 978–0-5572–1987-2) Proper of the Old Catholic Mass (2009)

The Complete Liturgy for Independent, Mystical and Liberal Catholics (ISBN 978–1-4538–4024-5) (2008)

The Divine and Healing Path by Bishop Elijah (ISBN 978–0557174249) (2010)

The Rites of the Old Catholic Church (ISBN 978–1452856919) (2009)

www.HeckIfIKnow.com
www.WynnWagnerBooks.com
www.MysticWaysBooks.com

Printed in Great Britain
by Amazon

61151028R00084